A private view

Left to right: Elisabeth Frink, David Wolfers, Rodrigo Moynihan and Robert Buhler in Dieppe, *c.*1952

A private view
David Wolfers and the New Grafton Gallery

Compiled by Julian Halsby

Lund Humphries

First published in 2002 by
Lund Humphries
Gower House
Croft Road
Aldershot
Hampshire
GU11 3HR

and

131 Main Street
Burlington
VT 05401
USA

www.lundhumphries.com

Lund Humphries is part of Ashgate Publishing

British Library Cataloguing-in-Publication Data
A catalogue record for this book is available from the British Library

Library of Congress control number: 2002110472

ISBN 0 85331 872 7

The author and the publisher have made every effort to trace the copyright holders or
owners of works and photographs. If any institutions or individuals have been incorrectly
credited, or if there have been any omissions, we would be glad to be notified so that the
necessary corrections can be made in any reprint.

Designed by Chrissie Charlton and Company
Typeset by Tom Knott in Monotype Van Dijck and Adobe Franklin Gothic Demi
Project managed by Rose James
Printed in Singapore under the supervision of MRM Graphics

Introduction

This book, *A Private View*, is about my father, David Wolfers. It contains his recollections of over fifty years in the art world, and of his creation of the New Grafton Gallery.

When I was about eighteen years old I asked my father to make a written record for me of his memoirs and the story of his gallery life; the book was to be called *No Moss* and originally it was intended to be a private journal, written just for me. Over some twenty years this idea went through various stages of development and waves of enthusiasm, but my father was too busy with the day-to-day running of the gallery to write it himself. However, he did not want to abandon the project, so in 1999 he asked his friend Julian Halsby to help him complete the task.

Together they compiled a history of the New Grafton Gallery, based on material stored in its archives, interspersed with his own memories and anecdotes. The book was nearly finished when my father died suddenly and unexpectedly, on 30 December 2001. Julian collated all the material gathered during their many meetings and recorded conversations, and so we have here, in David's own words, the story of how he came to launch and sustain the New Grafton Gallery.

David's life outside the art world is only lightly touched upon, as he always kept his private life separate from his business. However, the New Grafton Gallery did indeed reflect his personality, most of all his taste and his discerning eye.

I have always thought that there is a strong similarity between directing a gallery and publishing: just as a publisher chooses his authors and tends to be associated with certain kinds of books, so each reputable gallery has its own style, and is known for its owner's choice of artists and the character of its exhibitions. Consistently true to his beliefs, David Wolfers' great achievement was in opening a window onto the last fifty years of English painting, and visitors to the gallery were never disappointed in the nature and quality of the works they found on show.

David had a vivid personality. He was an attractive, generous-spirited man whose life was filled with many friendships, meetings and partings, ups and downs. He was married four times, but remained on good terms with all the women in his life. One of his favourite possessions was a 'Biographical Frame' containing photographs of himself from the age of nineteen until the present day, and including all four wives! Since his death, many friends, artists, collectors, critics and dealers have recalled their affection for him and their gratitude for all his endeavours. They have told me a great deal about my father and his work and how grateful they are for his help, encouragement and support.

He will long be remembered, and his presence will be greatly missed by many, especially by me, his only daughter. As his 'Saturday girl' in the gallery (self-appointed at the tender age of six) I first became aware of the art world and all its intricacies. My father influenced me and taught me everything I know: primarily to follow and to trust my eye, and always to believe in supporting and promoting true talent.

Although the art world has experienced many changes over the years, it is still a fascinating place to work. The New Grafton Gallery hosts a large family of artists and friends. Throughout the decades and all the changes, we have consistently mounted twelve exhibitions a year, never fearing the new. Growing up in the gallery world has taught me to expect nothing, and to enjoy everything. My father believed that 'Man does not live by bread alone': both his life and work were enriched by his abiding interest in art and his talent for friendship.

Although he is no longer here, the show still goes on. I miss his presence, but I realise how lucky I am to be David Wolfers' daughter and to be entrusted with the directorship of the New Grafton Gallery. His was a good life – we gave a party and the Gods all came.

Claudia Wolfers

Acknowledgements

Over a period of eighteen months I visited David Wolfers at his house in Barnes to talk about his years as a gallery man (he never liked to be called a dealer) and friend to many artists since the war. After a lengthy talk he would invite me to lunch at one of his favourite restaurants in Barnes, so compiling this book has been a pleasurable and interesting project. David's wife, Jacqueline, herself an artist and art restorer, has been most helpful and encouraged the project, especially at those times when David wondered whether anyone would be interested in his recollections.

The book could not have been written without the help of David's many friends and colleagues. Sarah Russell-Walling worked for sixteen years as his assistant and provided much information about David's relations with his artists. Tom Coates, Richard Pikesley, Mick Rooney, Ken Howard and Fred Cuming all gave of their time to meet me and talk about their years with the New Grafton, Tyrrell Young discussed the gallery from a collector's point of view, while Jeff Horwood told me about David's last trip to Dieppe with Ken Howard, Mick Rooney and himself, a 'jaunt' they called 'Four Men in a Merc'. Elfriede Windsor at Lund Humphries helped give the text focus and shape, and provided inspiring ideas for the title.

To all of these my thanks.

Julian Halsby

Biographical note

David Wolfers was born in 1917 in China, where he spent the first years of his life. His family found itself there because his maternal grandfather, Dr Charles Tenney, an American, had gone to that country as a missionary together with his young wife. They settled in the beautiful fishing village of Pai-Tai-Ho, which was later to become a famous beach resort, the 'St Tropez of China'. During his years there, Dr Tenney completely absorbed the Chinese way of life, even being converted to Confucianism. He wrote the first Chinese–English grammar, published by Macmillan, and founded a university. Towards the end of his life he was appointed as the American Minister in Peking, a rank equivalent nowadays to that of Ambassador.

David Wolfers' father worked in Tientsin as the manager of Arnhold Trading, an international trading company with American and English branches. His mother, Ruth Tenney, was a poet. A volume of her poems, including translations from Sappho, Lao Tzu and Hofmannstal was published in 1968 with an introduction by C.M. Bowra. The Wolfers family lived in considerable luxury with many servants, and enjoyed the full social life of expatriates.

When David was seven, he was sent to boarding school in Oxford; shortly afterwards his father was posted to the United States and all the family moved to a colonial-style house near Ossining on the Hudson River. Surrounded by woods and lakes, it was an ideal place for a teenager to grow up. David attended Kent School in Connecticut until he was fifteen, when his father was again transferred by the company, this time to London. David was sent to Radley, where he was a keen oarsman, representing the school at the Marlow and Henley regattas. From Radley he won an Exhibition to Worcester College, Oxford, to read PPE. At Oxford David worked, as he put it, 'moderately hard'. He took part in rowing, and also acted, playing Lysander in Shakespeare's *A Midsummer Night's Dream*. He was made President of the Lovelace Society, named after the Cavalier Sir Richard Lovelace, a poet who supported Charles I. On the outbreak of war in 1939, David enlisted with the Royal Artillery and was eventually posted to North Africa, serving with the Fourth Indian Division. He took part in the Battle of Sidi Barrani in

Deirdre Balfour (née Hart-Davis) *c.*1938

Geraldine Hill 1952

December 1940 and later fought the Germans at the Battle of Hellfire Pass and at Gazala, where he was wounded. He was awarded the Military Cross at Tobruk, where he was taken prisoner in 1942. He spent the rest of the war in POW camps; first in Italy where life was tolerable, but later in Czechoslovakia and Germany where conditions were very harsh. In April 1945, weighing just eight stone, he was repatriated to England.

The war over David, now aged twenty-eight, was offered a job as a trainee on the *Manchester Evening Chronicle*. In 1946 he married Deirdre Balfour and moved to London to work for the paper's Foreign Editor, Ian Fleming. After a period as London editor of the *Agence France Presse*, he was appointed Public Relations Officer for the International Chamber of Commerce in Paris and moved there with his wife, who was the niece of Duff Cooper, then British Ambassador to France. After six months in Paris, David applied for a job in the BBC and became producer of 'Home Talks' at Broadcasting House in Portland Place. He was also responsible for talks on *Woman's Hour* and found himself working with Basil Taylor, who was in charge of arts. David reviewed a number of exhibitions at the Victoria and Albert

Museum and also the 1948 *Battersea Open Air Exhibition of Sculpture*, where he first met Barbara Hepworth. In 1949 he was moved to Bush House, where his new job was to review the world press in a series of fifteen-minute broadcasts.

In 1956, some six years after the end of his first marriage, David married Joy Matthews, the Women's Editor of the *Daily Express*. This union was short lived and in 1960 he was married, for the third time, to Geraldine Hill, a journalist and public relations executive. Their only daughter, Claudia, was born in 1961. This marriage was dissolved after twenty years and in 1992 he married Jacqueline Taber, widow of the American artist Lincoln Taber and herself an artist and picture restorer.

David Wolfers died on 30 December 2001 aged 84. He had been honoured with a private lunch at Sotheby's shortly before his death and had worked in the gallery right up to the last days before Christmas, fulfilling his promise never to retire. His last exhibition was the most successful ever, selling eighty-four pictures.

For some years before his death David had been outlining an autobiography, and in late 1999 Julian Halsby embarked upon a series of interviews with him for a book on the history of the New Grafton Gallery. This account is in part a transcription of David's own words from these interviews.

The history of the New Grafton Gallery

David Wolfers

Early influences

My interest in art was first aroused during the Easter vacation at Oxford when I visited Paris for three weeks on a budget of £10. I visited the Louvre and saw David's *Victory of Samothrace* floodlit, a sight so moving that it brought tears to my eyes. I returned to Paris after the war when working for the International Chamber of Commerce. Paris seemed to have recovered from the war far more quickly than London, and I was able to visit many commercial galleries which were now back in business. I was disappointed, however, by what I saw in most of them: their heroes were Buffet and Dubuffet – artists that I do not find very interesting. I feel that the French suffer from the burden of such a remarkable heritage, which makes it very difficult for their contemporary artists.

Back in London working for the BBC, I was introduced to Basil Taylor, who was in charge of arts, and I was sent to cover the first *Battersea Open Air Sculpture Exhibition*; I also reviewed a number of other exhibitions. Thus both through work and socially, I was beginning to meet a number of artists. I met some members of the Royal College of Art (the RCA) staff in the early 1950s when Gilbert Spencer was Professor of Painting. In 1952 Robin Darwin took over as Rector and made radical changes to the staff, bringing in Carel Weight, Ruskin Spear, John Minton, Rodrigo Moynihan, Roger de Grey, Kenneth Rowntree and Colin Hayes. In a way it was Kenneth Clark who brought about this change acting behind the scenes as a kind of *éminence grise* in art education. He arranged for Darwin to take the RCA, and Coldstream the Slade while Gowing was sent to run Newcastle: Darwin was a great powerhouse who made the RCA what it is today.

The Moynihans and friends

In 1950 I met Rodrigo Moynihan, his wife Elinor Bellingham-Smith and his friends, including John Minton. The contact was through Julia Strachey, a niece of Lytton Strachey, who had a flat above me in Oakley Street. She was a good writer, although with a small output, and had written two novels: she also reviewed books for the *New Statesman*. Her first husband was the sculptor Tommy Tomlin who did the head of Lytton Strachey in the Tate. She spent the war with Lawrence Gowing who, as a conscientious objector, was allowed to paint. After the war Gowing became a tutor at Camberwell but he was soon appointed Head of Painting at Newcastle: he went up there, took up the post and had a fling with a young student whom he married, but the marriage lasted no time. Finally he married Julia, who was fifteen years his senior: I was a witness at the registry office marriage.

I felt at ease with the group, meeting them either at the Moynihans' rented house at 155 Old Church Street near the Chelsea Arts Club or going down to visit them in the country at Felstead, where Elinor's sister lived. Rodrigo had a studio at the college while Elinor painted in a room at home. Rodrigo, who was half Spanish, was an excellent conversationalist. He was a good professor of painting, building up an excellent team around him including Carel Weight, Colin Hayes and Robert Buhler. For the time he was an unconventional teacher, taking his students out to the pub, but he was very effective.

Rodrigo was also a good portrait painter and at the time I met him, he was working on a successful portrait of Clement Attlee. He was well paid for his work – for example £9000 for a portrait of the office machinery magnate, Gestetner. He also painted Princess Elizabeth, although this was not a great success. His *Portrait Group* of 1951 shows the newly appointed staff at the Royal College and is a fascinating record. He painted landscapes, although he later turned to abstraction, and before the war, he had been part of the English Surrealist Group. Rodrigo had a good eye for other painters' work and could talk well about art and artists. I remember him talking eloquently about Giacometti's work at the time of the London exhibition. David Sylvester, then critic for the *New Statesman*, was part of the group and his article about the exhibition was based on Rodrigo's conversation.

Elinor, who was rather beautiful, had met Rodrigo while they were both students at the Slade, where their contemporaries were William Coldstream, Geoffrey Tibble and Robin Darwin. She was also a good painter, working in a very different style from her husband, and I remember Philip Toynbee telling Rodrigo that his wife was the better painter. Her work was poetic and thoughtful, and her reputation as a painter has grown since her death. She mostly exhibited at the Leicester Galleries. In an article about her work in the *Tatler* of February 1959 I wrote:

> *The bare country of Essex and Suffolk blends well with a sense of poetic melancholy which finds its finest expression in her winter landscapes. At a time when so many painters are obsessed with the grotesque and the terrifying aspects of our age, she continues to find beauty in English landscape, even if this beauty seems at times to move her almost to tears.*

Their marriage was stormy at times; Rodrigo left her after twenty-five years for Ann Dunn, a wealthy lady who had a flat in New York and a house near Aix-en-Provence. Rodrigo went to live with her and even left the Royal Academy for a time. In 1957 Elinor retired to a house in Suffolk and rather dropped

Elinor Bellingham-Smith *Grassy Field* c.1954 oil on canvas 50 x 60 cm 20 x 24 in

out of the mainstream, although we continued to show her work in mixed exhibitions. We held a memorial show of Elinor's work in Barnes in 1989 with a dinner afterwards attended by Rodrigo and their son John Moynihan, who is a journalist.

Rodrigo was earning good money from his painting and teaching. As an impoverished journalist on a meagre salary of £1000 from the BBC I found it quite difficult keeping up with them; but I would join the group for drinks in the West End. A favourite spot was the Gargoyle Club in Frith Street, which was owned by David Tennant. It was on the first floor but it had low ceilings and felt like a basement. It had been going for some time and H.G. Wells had been an early habitué. It was a meeting place for painters and writers, and we would often bump into Cyril Connolly and Philip Toynbee. Another venue was the Colony Room which Francis Bacon and Lucian Freud frequented. This was a tiny room situated on the first floor and run by Muriel Belcher, who was a great character, and her girl friend Carmel Stewart. Muriel made me a life member. I remember meeting Henrietta Morais there, she was a rather rude lady; another member was the composer Isabelle Lambert.

Through Moynihan I met Johnny Minton, a charming man who was part of the famous Minton family of potters, and like Ruskin Spear, was a bit of a drinker. I remember going to Rodrigo's inaugural lecture when he was appointed Professor of Painting at the College. He took as his theme Chardin's *Les Attribues des Arts* at the Royal Society of Arts, after which we went out to eat in a little restaurant near Charing Cross. The group included Johnny Minton, Ruskin Spear, Francis Bacon and the Moynihans. At the time Bacon was quite unknown but I remember Ruskin Spear saying 'I think there's quite a nice streak in you, Bacon'.

I would sometimes meet Bacon at Wheeler's in Old Compton Street, where the group often dined. At this time his fame was just beginning. He had a contract with the Marlborough Gallery whereby they sent him a monthly cheque and took three or four paintings in return. Francis liked the regular cheque and used much of it to gamble in Monte Carlo. He was always very charming, friendly and unsnobby, even when he had become famous and rich. He was completely genuine. I once visited his studio and have never seen such a terrific mess. I admire his paintings, without actually wanting to own one. I think the key to his work is the fact that he was in Hitler's Germany before the war where he saw vice and corruption – this impregnated his thinking and he had to get it out of his system. He often used to say that he painted on his nerves.

Minton had a private income and did not depend upon his salary from the college. He had a house in Apollo Place, Chelsea, near the river and I remember him as a very charming, generous and kind man. He was good to his students, who liked his marvellous sense of humour. I recall him giving a talk to the students about contemporary art with a bottle of brandy on the table in front of him. He started by

John Minton *Imaginary Classical Scene* 1941 pen and ink 30 x 45 cm 12 x 18 in

saying 'I should emphasise that what I'm saying is pre-Sylvestrian'. He was reconciled to being homosexual and I do not think that this was the cause of his suicide in 1957. He had been proposed for membership of the Royal Academy, but the President Gerald Kelly strongly objected on the grounds of his homosexuality, despite the fact that the Academy was at the time showing the drawings of Michelangelo! I think his depression stemmed from his inability to be considered an important painter. For example he regarded his *Death of Nelson* as a serious work, but the public continued to see him more as an illustrator, especially after his work for Elizabeth David's book *Mediterranean Cookery*. Rodrigo Moynihan and Anthony Lousada, who were the executors of his estate, asked me to write his biography. I thought about it quite carefully but decided that it was too difficult in view of the strict homosexual laws then in force. You could say that he was an impossible subject because witticisms flowed from him like a mountain spring; he was one of the most engaging and sizzling personalities I have ever known.

Robert Buhler *Grocer's Shop, Rogate*
c.1942 oil on board
39.5 x 50 cm 15¾ x 20 in

I enjoyed the company of Ruskin Spear who was great fun, even if he did have a rather crude sense of humour. He painted a portrait of Bernard Fergusson, Lord Ballantrae, a soldier who had fought with the Black Watch in Burma. The regiment invited Spear to the ceremonial unveiling, but he caused a stir by bringing along his mistress. He was a heavy drinker, mostly of whisky, which inevitably led to many indiscretions. He never had a one-man show at the gallery, but he did take part in mixed exhibitions and I also obtained many portrait commissions for him. He sometimes painted rather obvious portraits from photographs in newspapers and I feel that this damaged his reputation. This was something that Sickert did in his later years, and Spear of course worshipped Sickert's work.

Another close friend of Moynihan's was Robert Buhler, who often expressed firmly held opinions in a downright manner, and did not suffer fools easily. He could be caustic, but he also had a good sense of humour. He was born in London of Swiss parents and was educated in Switzerland. His mother ran a famous pâtisserie and café in Soho called 'Madame Buhler'. I found him excellent company and while he also liked his drink he was a good writer, often producing articles for the RCA student magazine. In October 1958 I wrote an article in the *Tatler* about Buhler's portraits:

> *Buhler is the antithesis of a literary painter. Unlike his friend Carel Weight, he abhors objects and*
> *backgrounds in a painting. His backcloth is always stark: nothing but the subject matters. There must*
> *be no distracting trimmings ... The character is all that counts.*

I found Buhler's early work excellent but later it became starker and, to my mind, less interesting. I showed his work in mixed exhibitions, but he was promoted quite late in his career by Austin Desmond. Although Buhler, Ruskin Spear and Moynihan were all taken up by different dealers, we remained friends throughout this period.

I met Roger de Grey through the College. He had been at Newcastle working under Gowing, but came to the RCA as deputy to Carel Weight when Carel succeeded Moynihan as Professor. He eventually left to head the City and Guilds School, where he did an excellent job. He was an inspired President of the Royal Academy who tried to bring in new people and modernise. Roger was later a good friend to the gallery and a great supporter.

Lawrence Gowing occasionally joined us. He moved from Newcastle to be Head of Painting at Leeds and then on to Chelsea as Head of Painting. He was very ambitious and had a great desire for power. He joined the staff of the Tate and tried to become Director but lost the job to Norman Reid. His work was strongly influenced by Cézanne but I am not a great admirer of his painting, and I am not sure that art and power go well together. However he was a good portrait painter and I liked his portrait of Lord Halifax. He achieved the recognition he wanted, eventually becoming a member of the Royal Academy and getting a knighthood.

While I was working at the BBC I was invited to stay with Barbara Hepworth and Ben Nicholson for a weekend. I was an admirer of their work and I came to like them very much as people. That weekend I bought a piece by each of them, spending my entire month's salary and having to live very frugally for the next four weeks!

I first met Elisabeth Frink through Rodrigo Moynihan; she had become part of the group of friends who met at The Queen's Elm pub near his house in Chelsea. Stephen Gardiner, Frink's biographer, has described the Queen's Elm:

> It was singularly dreary, inside and out, with the appearance of boring suburbia somewhere along the Great West Road. Its wide, ugly windows followed the turn of the corner into Fulham Road, and there was no hint of a smoky, mysterious interior atmosphere to attract the passing drinker.... At the Elm (as it was usually known) the colour was the people.

Those who frequented it included the Moynihans, Minton, Laurie Lee, Robert Buhler and Michael Gough, and it was here that I met Elisabeth in late 1951.

Elisabeth Frink *c.*1954

At the time I was very keen on Cassis, which I used to visit by train. I was going there in the summer of 1952 so I phoned Lis from Cassis to invite her to meet me in Dieppe on my way back from the South. She wanted to, but had no money: I arranged for my mother to lend her £10. We arrived in Dieppe with no hotel booked, so I asked a policeman where his compatriots from Paris would stay. He directed us to the Café du Champ des Oiseaux on the outskirts of Dieppe, which cost us £1 a day for as much food and wine as we could consume. We had a glorious ten days together in this hotel which was virtually in the country. While we were there Rodrigo Moynihan and Keith Critchlow – an expert on oriental art and architecture and later Professor at the RCA – joined us for a weekend. In 1954 Lis and I returned to France, staying with the Moynihans for a few days in the house which they had rented from Orovida Pissarro in the hills above Toulon, before going on to Cassis.

I was amazed that such a young (Frink was in her early twenties) and apparently simple girl could produce such powerful sculpture and drawings. I might even have felt slightly intimidated; certainly I never asked her about her work nor ventured any criticism. She never discussed her ideas, never talked about her early days, about school at the convent, or anything like that. She never looked back, any more than she considered herself important – just a person who had a great need to get ahead with her job of

Elisabeth Frink *Fox* 1968 watercolour
67.5 x 100 cm 27 x 40 in

Bust of David Wolfers by
Elisabeth Frink 1957 bronze

work, and not waste time – in fact she referred to herself as a 'workman'. She didn't talk about it – once done, she was impatient to get on to the next thing as soon as possible, always looking forward to getting on with a new idea.

At about this time she was beginning to exhibit her work with great success. She showed a Seated Figure at the first Battersea Open Air Sculpture Exhibition and she asked me to write a short piece for her forthcoming show at the Beaux Arts Gallery where three castings of a bird sculpture were sold, one to the Tate, one to the Arts Council and one to Benjamin Britten.

In the following January, Frink was shortlisted out of 3500 entries for a competition to sculpt *The Unknown Political Prisoner*. She was the youngest of twelve finalists and a photograph of her with John Rothenstein, Director of the Tate, appeared in the *News Chronicle*. She was seen holding a maquette of a seated man, a raven on his left wrist. Although the first prize was ultimately won by Reg Butler, Frink had achieved considerable recognition. Shortly after this, she began work on my portrait, a sensitive and affectionate work which was probably her most successful likeness. The head was not a commission, being done for pleasure and as a present. She was extremely quick; a sitting rarely lasted more than an hour: I think there were three sittings in all, at her studio in Park Walk, Chelsea and, of course, she always worked in plaster rather than in clay. It was exhibited at the Royal Academy in its plaster form before casting and David Sylvester wrote about it in *The Times*, where it was illustrated, saying that it 'showed a warm affection'.

My relationship with Elisabeth Frink lasted a couple of years. At the end of 1954 she was offered a solo exhibition at the St George's Gallery in Cork Street. I remember telling her in 1955 that I could never marry her, because one day she would be famous like Epstein and I did not want to be 'Mr Frink'. As she never considered herself important, she was stunned by the split. However we were to remain friends for the next forty years and she became a keen supporter of the New Grafton, providing drawings for the opening of the gallery in 1967 even though she was then with Waddingtons. I feel that I possibly recognised her extraordinary talent before most people, as I wrote in an article in the *Tatler* in June 1959:

> *She is a true artist, driven on by a compelling force. She has an innate understanding of wild animals and is able to capture their combination of grace and force. If she goes on developing and adds humanity and depth of feeling to the obvious strength of her talent, she will become a great sculptress – and she is already one of the best in the country.*

Land and *Catalyst*

I was beginning to get a bit bored with the BBC because there was very little opportunity for advancement or promotion – this was before television had started. I wrote to five large companies asking if they required any public relations, and to my amazement I got a telegram from Shell inviting me to an interview in the Strand. I got the job of Press and Publications Manager for Shell Chemicals and left the BBC in 1957. I was number two to Stephen Garrett, the Group PR Manager, and my job involved dealing with the press, radio and television, writing speeches for directors and later starting two magazines for the company – *Land* and *Catalyst*. What I most enjoyed was getting designers and artists to illustrate these publications. The principle of *Land* was to be objective and informative rather than directly promoting the company, rather like the films that Shell made in which the scallop, Shell's symbol, only appears at the very end. When directors of the industrial side of the business saw the success of *Land* they wanted a similar magazine, which we called *Catalyst*, devoted to the chemical industry.

Sometimes we would do a profile of a farm, which I would visit along with a photographer and an artist – and naturally we stayed at the best hotel. I had a wonderful designer called John Lewis, but I also

Ruskin Spear *Portrait of Carel Weight*
1984 oil on board 62.5 x 75 cm 25 x 30 in

worked with a number of painters whom I commissioned. These included Robert Buhler, John Nash, Michael Andrews, Elinor Bellingham-Smith and Olwyn Bowey. The first issue of *Land* had a marvellous watercolour of a ploughed field on the cover by Paul Nash, but we had complaints from a number of farmers that the furrows were not straight! I commissioned Michael Andrews to paint a chemical factory in Manchester, a picture which was praised by David Sylvester. Michael Andrews was a very slow painter and only produced a couple of pictures a year. He later introduced me to Paul Newland and David Remfry who were both to show at the New Grafton. Ken Howard, who was just out of the Royal College, also did some illustrations for me at this time. In addition to making contacts with artists through Shell, I also had the opportunity to visit the West End art galleries as our office was at 170 Piccadilly, above Jacksons, and in my lunch hour I would walk round the galleries in the area.

When the Shell Centre on the South Bank was complete, Shell Chemicals moved in. I suggested to the directors that they should commission pictures to hang on several floors and I managed to persuade them to buy works by Freddie Gore, Carel Weight and Olwyn Bowey. I went round to their studios to choose the pictures. I had greater difficulty in persuading them to buy an Elisabeth Frink sculpture for the boardroom, but eventually they reluctantly agreed to pay £200 for the work. I was also Chairman of the Shell Art Club, which held an annual competition with about 200 paintings being submitted. My job was to invite an artist to act as the judge and Freddie Gore and Carel Weight both agreed to do the job.

The President of the Club was John Loudon, Managing Director of the Shell Group, a very charming Dutchman. I was to write his speech welcoming the judge, and after the judge had announced the five winners we would have lunch on the twenty-third floor in a private dining room designed by Margaret Casson.

During this period I had also been writing some art criticism. I persuaded the editor of *The Field* to include some criticism in the magazine and I wrote a two page feature on the Royal Academy. I also did something on Picasso, although what they really wanted was articles about wildlife painters. One year I wrote an article critical of the Summer Exhibition and was told by the editor that the proprietor did not agree with my views. He only wanted reviews of exhibitions of horses and sporting pictures!

The articles I wrote for the *Tatler* were more interesting: I did a series on 'Portrait Painters of Today' which included Robert Buhler, Carel Weight, Claude Rogers and Sir William Coldstream. In 1959 I wrote about the sculpture of Elisabeth Frink as well as an article on gallery owners including Arthur Jeffreys, Dudley Tooth, the Gimpels, Oliver Brown, Helen Lessore and Rex Nankevell of the Redfern Gallery. In 1961–2 I was art critic for a short-lived magazine called *Topic*, an English version of *Time* magazine, and wrote about John Hoyland, Terry Frost, Ivon Hitchens and Patrick Heron. This was a weekly magazine and I had to visit many art galleries while writing the series. Looking back at some of the articles, I think that I did spot some emerging talent quite early on. For example, in an article in September 1960 entitled 'Art from four to forty pounds', I singled out Euan Uglow (a still life in oils for £40), Elisabeth Frink, Ceri Richards, Jeffrey Camp and Craigie Aitchison as good buys.

Establishing the gallery

By the mid-1960s I had become so involved with artists and art criticism that I began to think about running my own gallery. Two or three friends told me to have a go, as they knew that I had been wanting to do it for several years. It was a very difficult decision to leave a safe job with a reliable income to take the enormous risk of setting up on my own. I had a small pension from Shell and my wife Geraldine was working three and half days a week, so we could just scrape by. It was nevertheless a gamble, and most of my backers never expected to see their money returned. However I had been in Shell for eleven years and I was given a lump sum of £7000 as well as a small pension; in addition a number of people offered me money for the venture, so eventually I had about £9000 plus my Shell money. In fact my backers had their capital repaid after five years, and in addition, were given 10 per cent off any pictures they bought. To celebrate the clearing of the loan, I invited all the investors to a lunch at a private room at the Garrick.

Top left: John Nash at Wormingford *c.*1975
Top right: Sheila Fell *c.*1968
Bottom left: Reg Gammon *c.*1987
Bottom right: Edward Ardizzone

Alasdair Rennie *Saunton Sunset 2* 2002 oil on board 30 x 45 cm 12 x 18 in

I left Shell at the end of 1967 and began looking for premises that were not too expensive. Eventually I found a nice property at 1A Grafton Street, just near the corner of Hay Hill, which had been the Grafton Coffee House and later an estate agency called Pearsons. It was in a rather sorry state and in the basement we discovered seventeen gas stoves, all covered in grease! The landlords were Land Securities and the rent was £2000 per annum which was reasonable for the time. I decided to call the gallery the 'New Grafton' because Roger Fry had put on the first post-Impressionist show at the Grafton Galleries in 1910. The gallery had been bombed in 1941 and never reopened. Margaret Casson advised me about the interior design and on her suggestion we put gold hessian on the walls and a gold-coloured carpet to match. (She was the wife of Hugh Casson who at the time was Professor of Interior Design at the Royal College with Margaret as his senior tutor. We went on to show Hugh's watercolours very successfully.)

I signed the lease on 1 June and planned to open on 28 July, which was a very tight timetable. In the meantime I interviewed potential secretaries at Browns Hotel. My first question was always 'Do you smoke?' I chose Caroline, who had done an art course and had worked for *Harpers and Queen* as secretary to the art editor for two years. I was also lucky to have a part-time assistant who came for four hours a day, four times a week, which allowed me to get out of the gallery to see artists and clients. I had met Penny Boswell, who was married to Reggie Boswell, a sculptor who had studied at the Slade, on a train coming back from Brighton where I had been looking at a gallery for sale. We got into conversation and she asked me what I did. I replied that I was about to open a gallery and she said that she would love to work part time. When I phoned some weeks later she said 'Good heavens! I never expected you would actually do it. I thought it was just one of those fictional things.'

The gallery was ready on time and we held a party to which I invited virtually everyone I had ever met. One of the dealers I had visited in the area was Helen Lessore, who had the Beaux Arts Gallery. She said 'You can't possibly open at the end of July because nobody will be in London.' I replied that I started paying rent from 1 June and simply had to open. The opening was most encouraging: about 140 people attended and we sold most of the pictures. I had decided that the first person to buy a picture would be given a bottle of champagne – this turned out to be the head of Willis Faber, the insurance company. The opening show included works by Patrick George, Freddie Gore, Colin Hayes, Josef Herman, Ivon Hitchens, Helen Lessore, Ben Levene, L.S. Lowry, John Nash, John Piper, Ruskin Spear, Carel Weight and Gilbert and Stanley Spencer. Thus on 28 July 1968 the New Grafton Gallery was established, my new life as a gallery man began, and an enjoyable and fruitful partnership between the gallery, artists, clients and friends was established.

In the early years many people were most helpful, not with money but with advice. For instance Victor Waddington, who had his own little 'retirement' gallery as he called it, was extremely helpful and gave good advice, even lending me one or two Jack Yeats paintings. Helen Lessore was also a great supporter and introduced me to a number of painters including Ben Levene, who became one of my first artists. I also had some good luck and one of my first big customers was Andrew Carnwath, Managing Director of Barings Bank. He used to arrive, look at a painting for about ten minutes (the first one I think was a Hitchens), and say that he would have it. There was no beating around the bush. He bought several paintings, some for Barings and some for himself. He had a very good eye. Julie Lawson, secretary of the ICA, brought Roland Penrose along to the opening. He had a magnificent collection of works by Matisse and Picasso and commented that my opening show was 'very good of its kind'.

The gallery was charming. It had a minstrels' gallery upstairs where I showed eighteenth- and nineteenth-century watercolours, while downstairs was dedicated to twentieth-century artists, of which some 80 per cent were alive and working. In my first catalogue I set out what I was planning to do, but after three years I decided to opt out of the eighteenth and nineteenth centuries and concentrate solely on the twentieth century. We originally held some sculpture shows including exhibitions of Chaim Stephenson in 1968 and Vincent Butler in 1969, but we decided that the space was too small to show sculpture to its best advantage. Later we showed only portrait sculpture and drawings for sculpture.

Every year I used to have a show of English painting and drawing 1900–1940, including works by Gilbert and Stanley Spencer, John and Paul Nash, Henry Lamb, Spencer Gore, the Camden Town School and occasionally Sickert. In those days they were relatively cheap but I did not have the capital to keep them, even though today they would be worth twenty times as much. However, one cannot think like that. On one occasion Jocelyn Herbert, who was an old friend, asked me if I would be interested in a large Stanley Spencer. I said that I certainly would and she replied that Michael Marks had one he wanted to sell. Marks was the son of the Marks and Spencer family but had little interest in the firm, preferring to run puppet shows. So he brought it in and we went to Tooth's, which had been Spencer's gallery, for a valuation. It was a portrait of Spencer's maid Elsie standing in front of a bookcase. They said that £3000 was a fair price for it, although it was the most I had ever paid for a painting. Within an hour of the picture being in the gallery, Anthony D'Offay came round with James Kirkman, who was at the Marlborough, and bought it for £4000. I had made £1000, which was very nice, but today it would be worth over £100,000. I also had a good Sickert picture *Ethel Sands Descending a Staircase* which I sold to Wolverhampton Art Gallery. For the gallery this annual show was important, because it made real money.

Capital was always a problem as I had to buy pictures at auction. I had no private means so it was a bit of a struggle. A merchant bank offered to lend me £15,000 but on the condition that one of their young men could go through my books once a month. I felt that this was a loss of liberty so I declined. I set up a scheme whereby I would buy pictures jointly with other investors. Two or three people joined the scheme including Andrew Carnwath, who lent me money in order to buy Sickert's picture of

Gilbert Spencer *Early Self Portrait* (detail) 1928
oil on canvas 35 x 30 cm 14 x 12 in
© Courtesy of the artist's estate/Bridgeman Art Library

Gilbert Spencer *The Miller* 1928
oil on canvas 178.75 x 123 cm 71½ x 49¼ in

Henry Lamb *Lytton Strachey* (detail) 1914
oil on canvas 50 x 40 cm 20 x 16 in
© Tate, London 2002

Henry Lamb *Portrait of Evelyn Waugh* 1930
oil on canvas 73.75 x 61.25 cm 29½ x 24½ in

Keith Vaughan *Kneeling Nude* c.1962 gouache 45 x 41.25 cm 18 x 16½ in

Ethel Sands. The scheme worked well and, assuming I sold the picture within 12–15 months, the investors would get a good return. Unlike many gallery owners, I never had a sleeping partner to provide finance and once I had repaid my original backers, I never borrowed money. I had no obligations to others and I remained independent.

One of the first shows at the gallery was 'The Nude' for which Kenneth Clark wrote a short foreword to the catalogue. The English are rather shy about buying nudes and say 'Oh what a beautiful painting but I don't think I could have it in my drawing room'. They go and look at nudes in museums but rarely buy them. However we got a very good press for the show and the workmen working outside used to peer through the window and giggle. The exhibition included paintings by Euan Uglow, Christopher Wood, John Nash, Bernard Dunstan, Josef Herman and Philip Sutton.

Another successful theme for an exhibition was 'Vanishing London' which we held in 1972. There was an excellent Robert Buhler of Piccadilly Circus in 1947, a Carel Weight of Campden Hill in 1944 and a Ruskin Spear of Hammersmith Bridge in 1953. Other artists included Sir Hugh Casson, Ken Howard, John Ward, Christopher Hall and Diana Armfield. In the early years the Press was kind to the gallery. Marina Vaizey wrote a long article in the *Financial Times* to mark the tenth anniversary of the gallery and Terence Mullaly would review one exhibition in three in the *Daily Telegraph*. He shared a similar taste to mine and liked figurative painting.

When the gallery was about three years old, I decided to start a Portrait Centre with some sixteen portrait painters and five sculptors, all of whom would leave examples of their work and photographs for anybody wanting a portrait to examine. It has proved a good bread and butter line, something that has helped pay the rent and on average we commission 10–12 portraits a year. The commissions range from modest drawings to expensive oils by well-established artists. I try to match the artist to the sitter, to find an artist whose style and approach I consider suitable for the sitter's portrait. If someone comes to me and says they want a portrait of great aunt Dolly who is ninety-three, I would be able to suggest an artist who is good at painting older people. Some painters are better at rugged features than soft feminine complexions, while others prefer children to adults. In an article in the *Financial Times* to mark our fifth anniversary in 1973, Marina Vaizey wrote about the Portrait Centre: 'People can look at a wide range of accomplished, intelligent and incisive portrait painting, paintings of character, untouched by flattery or smudgy sentimentality, and get an idea about what kind of portrait they might like to commission'.

On one occasion I wrote to Prudence Glynn, Fashion Editor of *The Times*, suggesting that she have her portrait painted by three of our artists whom she could choose. She agreed and devoted a whole page to the project. Later she held a reception at the gallery, the champagne provided by Moët et Chandon, to which she invited all the leading designers like Jean Muir. Another highlight was Angela Connor, who had sculpted Lucian Freud, Harold Macmillan, the Duke of Devonshire and John Betjeman. We arranged a buffet lunch at the gallery for the press and displayed a number of her portraits. The press arrived in large numbers because they knew that Harold Macmillan, then aged eighty-six and no longer Prime Minister, would be coming. We had arranged a card table to be set up in the gallery where my wife sat with the three 'elder statesmen', Harold Macmillan, John Betjeman and Harold Caccia who had been head of the Foreign Office. Macmillan was a charming guest. *The Times* Diary carried a long piece the following day.

Another important visitor to the gallery was the Duke of Edinburgh, who came to see one of the three exhibitions we held of Reynolds Stone, a painter as well as an engraver and lettering expert who had designed bank notes and the stationery for the Royal Family. The Duke of Edinburgh talked to Reynolds Stone for ten minutes or so on how to do wood engraving, then asked me how I ran a gallery. Stone's wife, Janet, said she would stay hidden in my office, as she didn't want to steal the limelight, but she couldn't resist and was introduced to the Duke.

In 1973 I had a letter from the Australian Cultural Attaché asking me if I would like to have a show by one of the leading Australian painters, Lloyd Rees. He sent me a book about his work and I was rather taken by it. Rees had never shown in England before but came over for the exhibition with his wife. The exhibition was opened by the Australian High Commissioner, who made a short speech and was followed by Barry Humphries, who did a brilliant take-off of the High Commissioner's speech. Rees' pictures were expensive by my standards at the time, between £2000 and £7000, and he was unknown in this country. We only sold ten, mostly to Australians, and he was very upset by the poor sales. In Australia he was considered the grand old man of Australian art and he died a few years ago aged ninety-three.

At this time I used to meet Matthew Smith and have lunch with him. He was a delightful man who had a flat in Sloane Avenue. He had gone very late to the Slade, aged about forty, but had no circle of close friends. He was always quite formal and well dressed in a suit. His sons had been in the RAF during the war, and both had been killed. He was something of a loner, although he had both a wife and a mistress. I remember meeting him one day when he was off to visit his wife and his mistress who were, by chance, both in the same hospital. 'I'm off to hospital', he said 'to kill two birds with one stone'. I was a great admirer of his work, but we never had the opportunity to exhibit his pictures.

The move to Bond Street

The lease at Grafton Street was renewable every five years and at the end of the first term we got notification from the landlords that they planned to demolish the west side of Hay Hill and build an apartment block with a penthouse for the company's chairman, Lord Samuel. It would have been a scandal to do this and I helped organise resistance with about eight of my neighbours. We finally won and shared the legal costs, and I was able to stay in the gallery at the same rent for another two and a half years. The landlords then decided to refurbish the premises which took another eighteen months. Finally they tripled my rent and after eight successful years in Grafton Street I realised that we had to move.

We had a part-time secretary whom I asked to look out for suitable premises. She discovered that the floor above Agnews in Bond Street had been vacant for eighteen months and was available at a rent of £5500. It was a large premises which didn't need much doing to it, just laying a carpet and dividing off the front room to turn it into a storage space for pictures. There was also enough room for a tiny office at the back where confidential business could be done in private. The main disadvantage was that it was on the first floor, but as I had by then built up a clientele I decided to take it. Only rarely did people come in off the street to buy and our mailing list was the backbone of the gallery. However we did put up a board at street level saying 'New Grafton Gallery on the First Floor'. The space was good although the gallery was less attractive than our previous one, in particular the lighting, but as I only had a five year lease, I was reluctant to spend money on the fittings.

We held some successful shows in Bond Street including 'Orovida Pissarro and her Ancestors' in 1977 which included work by her grandfather, Camille, and father Lucien Pissarro. We were lent four Camilles as well as about ten Luciens. The Camilles were not for sale, alas, as even then they would have been worth up to half a million pounds. Of the Lucien Pissarros we sold only three; but we did sell many of Orovida's excellent etchings. The show also generated quite a lot of publicity. Inevitably the art world attracts famous names and we had our fair share in the gallery. I remember Graham Greene who bought a picture from a show by the Polish artist Zdzislaw Ruszkowski. He bargained over the price but finally paid £250 for it. When he came to London he always stayed at the Ritz, which was near the gallery.

Agnews have owned their premises since around 1900 and had only rates and no rent to pay. Their property was managed by Hamptons who decided that my rent should be tripled, in addition to a doubling of the rates. I tried to negotiate but Hamptons were adamant, so we had to arrange to decamp and relet the property, which still had a couple of years left on the lease.

Peter Greenham, RA Schools 1975

Cyril Reason, Helen Roeder, Carel Weight and Mick Rooney at the New Grafton Gallery, 1993

Mick Rooney, David Wolfers, Ken Howard at Varengeville, 2001

Barnes

I decided to move to Barnes as I had been living there for eighteen years and a well-situated property, near the pond and with easy parking, became available. Some people thought Barnes was as remote as the Hebrides, but in fact it is just over Hammersmith Bridge, and having had fifteen years in the West End I felt that we were established enough to make the move. In fact about 80 per cent of our customers followed us and in addition we acquired new ones from south-west London. Saturdays are always much livelier here than in the West End and it has become our busiest day. However, if I had started the gallery in Barnes and tried to move to the West End, I think it would have been much more difficult. I live about 500 yards from the gallery and it is a real advantage to be able to walk to work. The gallery was launched with a big party and June Robinson, the mayor at the time, agreed to officiate at the opening. The press attended and photographs were taken.

Many artists approach the gallery, but most are not my taste. I believe that a successful gallery must have a recognisable and consistent personality which is reflected in the choice of work. I look for a combination of good technique and a sense of originality and I avoid pictures which depend upon gimmicks. I'm not prepared to sell pictures just in order to make money. When I was in the West End people would come in and offer me Russell Flints, and even though they would sell easily I wouldn't touch them. A gallery becomes a bazaar if you show anything you think will sell.

Art dealing is not just about making money: there are many far easier ways of earning money than running a gallery. I think I realised this long before I opened the New Grafton, when I wrote in an article about the economics of art galleries in *The Director* in November 1962: 'Art dealing seems to be more than a means of making money. It has become a profession practised with care and affection for its own sake.' I once talked to Dudley Tooth, who for years ran one of the most important galleries in the West End, and he told me that to him being an art dealer was just like being a stockbroker. It's certainly not like that for me.

Many art dealers do things differently from me; for example they will buy pictures back at auction to keep the prices high. I consider the New Grafton to be an art gallery, as opposed to an art dealership, because I do not speculate and try to create false markets in an artist's work. Occasionally I go to the saleroom to buy pictures by artists whose work we have sold over the years, but this forms a very small part of the business.

The New Grafton has done much to encourage young artists, possibly more than any other London gallery, and we use our regular mixed exhibitions as a way of introducing their work to the public. Nothing gives me more pleasure than sending artists, especially young artists, cheques. I have regularly attended Final Shows at the Royal Academy Schools and many of my younger artists have come from that source. Under Peter Greenham it was one of the few art schools that encouraged drawing, but in recent years it has become more trendy and more like Goldsmiths.

Artists have to stick to their last, hoping to sell rather than painting in order to sell. There is always the danger that they will continue to churn out the same picture simply to sell. Life is more difficult for figurative artists today because in the past many had jobs in art colleges, either full- or part-time, and were not obliged to rely upon their picture sales in order to live. I think that the Coldstream Report did great damage in combining art schools with polytechnics and placing emphasis upon pseudo-academic training; as a result there are very few part-time posts for representational painters. I understand that artists have to achieve the highest prices they can for their work, and to do that they sometimes leave the New Grafton. However, I also find this upsetting, especially if we have established a good relationship with the artist and built up a clientele for their work. A gallery has to have big names whose shows always sell well, because other exhibitions often do not make money.

I think that post-war British art is amongst the best in Europe and that artists such as Spencer, Moore, Frink, Freud, Bacon, Burra and Weight have few rivals abroad. I am not so sure about Brit-art, as I feel it is based largely on publicity and gimmickry. An artist like Damien Hirst is a master of self-publicity, but whether his work will stand the test of time is another matter. It does not make me angry because my public continue to like traditional painting and suggestions that painting is dead are simply untrue.

Patrick Heron *December 6: 1983* 1983 gouache on paper   34.5 x 48.75 cm   13¾ x 19⅝ in

Gus Cummins *The Long Man, Wilmington* 1993 oil on board 20 x 15 cm 8 x 6 in

Jason Bowyer *The Garden Hibiscus* 1991 oil on canvas 37.5 x 42.5 cm 15 x 17 in

John Armstrong *Three Philosophers* *c.*1971 oil on canvas 55 x 75 cm 22 x 30 in

Running a gallery has changed over the last forty years; today there is much more emphasis upon high profile and public relations, although the New Grafton has never employed a public relations company. Ultimately it's about looking at pictures and trying to understand them: it is about quality, not theory and publicity. Many years ago I was talking to Francis Bacon about David Sylvester, the doyen of post-war art critics in Britain. I remember saying to Bacon 'I think David Sylvester is blind. He doesn't look at a picture; he evolves a theory about it'. Bacon replied 'You know I've always thought that, but you're the first person to actually say it.'

I consider myself very lucky to be doing what I want for a living and I have made many lifelong friends through the gallery. I might drop dead, but I'll never retire.

Pip Todd Warmoth *Two Camel Riders* 2000 oil on board 85 x 90 cm 34 x 36 in

Mary Jackson *Felucca on the Nile* 2002 oil on board 30 x 35 cm 12 x 14 in

Anthea Craigmyle *Fatima and the Cat* 2000 oil on canvas 30 x 40 cm 12 x 16 in

Artists of the New Grafton Gallery

Peter Greenham *Life Class at the Byam Shaw* 1979 oil on canvas 43.75 x 67.5 cm 17½ x 27 in
© Courtesy of the artists estate/Bridgeman Art Library
© Tate, London 2002

Peter Greenham is an interesting figure in post-war painting, a portrait and landscape artist who was also an inspired Keeper of the Royal Academy, in effect director of the Royal Academy Schools. He remained an academic and somewhat retiring man, but greatly admired by his pupils at the RA Schools, and in his quiet way he ran the Schools extremely well. The students were encouraged to draw for the first year which was unusual even then, and he believed that drawing from life was a good discipline and the basis for good painting. Under his direction the schools were a very happy place to work.

I first met Greenham through Carel Weight when I was starting the Portrait Centre, and found him diffident but very charming. When I got to know him rather better, I suggested that he might like to hold an exhibition of his non-portrait work. He was already into his fifties but had never held a one-man show, having depended on the steady support of a group of patrons. After some hesitation he agreed to a show which took place in 1972. One day shortly before the opening he rang me, worried that if he sold all his pictures he would have nothing to leave to his wife, Jane Dowling. I tried to reassure him that an exhibition would further his reputation and increase his prices in the salerooms. This first exhibition was mostly of landscapes, many painted around Lake Annecy which he visited most years, sometimes accompanied by his pupil from the Schools, Edmund Fairfax-Lucy. The show was nearly a sell out, but I had another call from Peter, worrying about what he should do with the money. He wanted to invest for his children's education and I introduced him to Simon Birch, a stockbroker who wisely suggested that he should not speculate but put the money into a building society.

By the time of the first show in 1972 Peter was already Keeper of the Academy and I visited his flat at Burlington House. This was situated on the second floor above the Friends office and consisted of a large studio with a place to sleep and a bathroom. He loved music and had a piano in the flat. He took his duties as Keeper very seriously although he never asked for a salary rise, feeling that he should not take money from the Academy. He was a formal person, always well-dressed, and it took me about three years to get to know him, during which he always addressed me as 'Wolfers'. Eventually he began to call me David and I even plucked up enough courage to call him Peter. He was slow to become a friend, but when he did he was firm and loyal, and when I moved the gallery from Bond Street to Barnes he didn't leave me. He could have joined Agnews or any other gallery, but he stuck with me which was typical of his loyalty. When he died in 1992 I felt the loss, not only of a very fine painter, but also of a good friend.

Peter was an excellent portrait painter and I got him a number of commissions. He was a slow worker and would often go on and on working on a portrait, in one case for nearly three years. I decided that it would be best to give him a deadline of twelve months, but even so he would require endless sittings which would take place each month at his studio in the Academy. He would often work on several portraits of the same sitter at the same time. He did three superb portraits of Lady Charlotte Bonham Carter and an outstanding one of an elderly Catholic priest, Father D'Arcy. His best portraits were of older people whose faces were full of lines and character. He found that younger faces reflected a lack of experience in life and were less interesting to paint.

Not all his portraits worked, and sometimes he would even give up. The one of Edward Heath in the Carlton Club is not, in my view, a great success although it hangs alongside all the other Conservative Prime Ministers from Disraeli onwards. Heath had a rather fleshy face and Peter was much better at faces with more angular features. Another commission which was not a total success was that of Asa Briggs for Worcester College, Oxford. I thought it was good, but Lady Briggs said the mouth was wrong. He also painted Isaiah Berlin for New College. I consider it to be an excellent painting, although Sir Isaiah apparently did not like it.

We held six one-man shows of Peter Greenham's work, with a further two shared with Jane Dowling and a memorial exhibition in 1993. At the 1975 exhibition in Bond Street the Tate Gallery bought a large painting called *The Life Class at the Byam Shaw*. He had taught at the Byam Shaw and had been working on this picture for nearly twenty years. Richard Morphet from the Tate was a fan of his work and I know that Peter was pleased that the Tate bought it.

Three weeks before the 1979 show Peter wrote to me saying that he did not have enough work. I replied with a postcard of St Sebastian pierced with arrows, saying that he was the martyred saint. We managed to postpone the exhibition until he had enough pictures. His exhibitions never had a theme: he would show landscapes, interiors and some informal portraits. He usually painted outside on the spot and many of his pictures are quite small, although he also did larger works in the studio. He loved the Norfolk coast, often painting beach scenes at Mundesley, and also worked in Oxfordshire where he lived, while his summer trips to France provided further inspiration. An important artist who never attempted to be fashionable, his work has great integrity and originality with a touch of poetry, both in the subject and in the handling of the paint. The reason that he is not better known is probably that he never produced enough work.

He was a craftsman who always put his oils under glass to give the paint time to settle before varnishing. He was also rather fussy about his frames and evolved his own style of framing with the help of Terry Burns at Academy Framing. He was scholarly and enjoyed art history, writing a book about Velázquez,

Mark Adlington *Roe in Velvet* 1998 mixed media on paper 150 x 200 cm 60 x 80 in

Elisabeth Frink *Dog* 1988 watercolour and pencil on paper 70 x 60 cm 28 x 24 in

one of his heroes. He had a number of friends at the Academy including Carel Weight, Walter Woodington, Richard Eurich, Kyffin Williams, Colin Hayes and Bernard Dunstan, but I think he would have been shocked and disappointed by the recent development of the Academy Schools. After he was elected an RA, Robin Darwin wrote a report on the Schools proposing many changes: Peter wrote a marvellous reply challenging many of his assumptions.

Peter's wife, Jane Dowling, also exhibited with us. Like Peter she studied at Oxford, at St Anne's College, before going on to the Slade, Byam Shaw and the Central School. Her work is sometimes whimsical with a very unusual way of looking at life. She often paints scenes of rural England, the beach at Mundesley and of course France where they both worked. Peter used to worry about how Jane's sales were going, and while he never telephoned to ask about his own shows, he was always on the phone when his wife was exhibiting. I think her role as a teacher at the Royal Academy Schools and at the Ruskin in Oxford has been important and she has certainly been an influence on the revival of tempera painting.

One of the most important and successful shows to be held at the New Grafton in Barnes was the 1989 retrospective of drawings by **Elisabeth Frink**. We remained friends after her marriage to Michel Jammet in 1955, but the marriage was dissolved in 1963 and Lis then married Ted Poole, moving to France to live near Nîmes in 1967. During her nine years in France we saw much less of each other but we remained in contact. I think she felt cut off: artists need criticism and contact with the art world and it is difficult to live in a vacuum. After her marriage to Alex Csaky in 1974 they bought a house in Dorset, Wolland House near Blandford, dating back to the sixteenth century. Alex could breed horses and Lis work in her studio. We were regular visitors. The studio was wonderful and there were sculptures around the gardens and swimming pool. It was an idyllic life and she used to ride regularly; her father had been a jockey and cavalry officer and she had been brought up with horses. On one occasion an intruder got in and killed some of the horses and Lis did a series of drawings, which we showed at the gallery, of horses' heads covered in blood.

In the 1989 Frink retrospective of drawings we also showed three maquettes of a water buffalo. Her drawings were extremely strong and were much more than just working sketches, often having watercolour washes. Our clients admired them and they were easy to sell. This was the first retrospective of her drawings ever held – I pushed the boat out in terms of advertising and I even had posters printed for the Tube and public places. It was very nearly a sell-out and as the pictures were quite expensive, by my standards at least, the show was a great financial success. At the same time Lis had a sculpture exhibition at Fischer Fine Art and one of lithographs and screen prints at Lumley Cazalet, so it was a big bang with all three being launched at the same time.

Ruskin Spear CBE RA *Green Light* 1961 oil on board 30 x 37.5 cm 12 x 15 in

My daughter Claudia had got to know her well and Lis asked Claudia to take her over to Paris to see the Matisse Exhibition in March 1993, not long before she died. She told her that she wanted to 'say goodbye to Matisse' and Claudia took her round the exhibition in a wheelchair, a bandanna round her head as she had lost her hair through chemotherapy. I met them at London Airport on their return and drove them to our house in Barnes. She stayed for a while but looked very ill. She said that I should come and stay soon, but she was obviously trying to keep up appearances. Claudia drove her back to Dorset and I was not really surprised when Lis died about ten days later.

I went to her memorial service at St James' Piccadilly and then a few months later there was a service in Salisbury Cathedral for Lis and her husband Alex, who died two months before her. There must have been over 200 people there to give her a good send off. She was an exceptional person who drove herself tremendously hard. She used to get up at six o'clock and start work before having a swim at eight o'clock, followed by breakfast before returning to work until after one. She really pushed herself and at the very end she had just completed an enormous *Risen Christ* which had been commissioned for Liverpool Cathedral. The plaster was finished in time, and the unveiling took place a few days before she died. She could not attend but her son, Lin, represented her.

Lis was an instinctive artist, who at first found it very difficult putting her ideas into words. With the help of Laurie Lee she got better at words, but she remained totally unspoilt. She supported Amnesty International all of her life, and her success in no way changed her. Her reputation continues to grow. She is perhaps less important than Hepworth or Moore but she comes a close third, and she will certainly hold an important place in the history of English art. She was only sixty-two when she died.

I got to know **John Nash** quite well in my days at Shell. I used to take an artist and a photographer when I went on a visit to a farm or agricultural merchant, and on a couple of occasions I took John with me. When I started the gallery I hoped that John might have a one-man show with us but he was already with Agnews; however he always let us have a few pictures.

Years later he wrote me a wonderful letter saying 'Dear David, I think I'll fall off my perch one of these days. I've got a great favour to ask you. Would you be my artistic trustee?' I was thrilled and wrote back saying that it would be a great honour and from then on I had more or less a monopoly of his work. In 1967 he was given a retrospective at the Royal Academy where he was a member, and I think the public began to realise just how good he was. There was an excellent introduction to the catalogue written by Freddie Gore.

John Nash was quintessentially English, quiet, musical, rather scholarly and well read. He was a real countryman, a keen fisherman, with a love of the English landscape, and was in fact an enthusiastic gardener, often drawing plants and flowers from his garden. He worked in watercolour as well as in oils, rather in the tradition of Samuel Palmer, of whom he was a great admirer. He really understood the countryside, and was fascinated by the marks left on the landscape by men – ploughmen, quarrymen, ditchers, china clay diggers, as well as old quarries, ponds, fences and ditches. Kenneth Clark had great respect for him and he was highly regarded in art academic circles, such as the Fitzwilliam and Ashmolean Museums. He had been in the Artists Rifles during the First World War and had painted in France. After the war he did some part-time teaching at the Royal College and at Colchester.

He was a delightful and modest man who lived in a charming seventeenth-century cottage at Wormingford on the Essex–Suffolk border. To get to the house you had to go through an orchard of greengage, quince and plum, and a stream ran past the house so there was always the sound of running water. His wife Christine was a good cook and I always enjoyed visiting them. He much preferred East Anglia to London, but when I was down there he would always say 'Now tell me about all the goings on in London'. He did not belong to any particular school or group of artists and was always his own man. I suppose he was influenced by his friends Bawden and Ravilious, but his brother Paul Nash was correct when he described John's paintings as 'the products of true naivety, as authentic as the Douanier Rousseau'. John was always overshadowed by the fame and success of Paul.

When he died in 1977, a few years after his wife, I cleared his small studio and took over his artistic estate which resulted in seven exhibitions, so he played a very big part in my gallery life. The first retrospective took place about a year after his death and I borrowed pictures from the Imperial War Museum and other important collections. He left his house to Ronnie Blythe, the writer and author of *Aikenfield*, who had first met Nash when he was sixteen and had often 'house sat' for him when he was away.

The first retrospective set out to represent all aspects of Nash's work including oils, watercolours, drawings and woodcuts. The *Observer* magazine did a feature and the *Sunday Times* also carried a piece on his work, while several art critics wrote articles. Some years after his death Rothenstein wrote a small book about his work and I was able to help with the illustrations. Ronnie Blythe wrote a very good foreword to the catalogue. The last paragraph read:

> *It was a countryside which John had known of, rather than known, since boyhood. In 1911 Paul had taken part in a pageant there and his Tudor costume lay folded away immediately below the studio. In 1929 John and his wife discovered it fully for themselves. A postcard of the village dated 1929 says 'Good river scenery – think we might stay here'. He depended upon conditions of Wordsworthian simplicity which, perhaps, can never again be so unselfconsciously achieved.*

John Aldridge was another artist in the English tradition who painted the landscape of East Anglia where he lived. I knew him while he was alive, but he did not show at the gallery until after his death when we organised his retrospective. He was a charming man, a gentleman, quiet, modest and polite, who always wore a suit and tie. I see him in the same spirit as John Nash and Edward Bawden. He was a great friend of Robert Graves and would stay in Majorca with him every summer. After his death his pictures were put into storage in the Hackney area and I went to the warehouse to select the pictures. He is totally out of fashion now, although the prices of his pictures in the salerooms are rising.

We gave **Cedric Morris** a retrospective in 1975 at a time when his work had been almost totally forgotten. I knew Cedric quite well and found him a very charming man, and a keen, even famous, gardener. He lived at Benton End with Lett Haines and rather turned his back on the London art scene, having enough money to live on. He was not ambitious; he just carried on painting whether he sold or not. They had a cook called Gracie who provided all their meals and he helped with the East Anglian School of Painting, which he had established in 1936 and which had a number of distinguished students including Maggie Hambling and Lucian Freud. He particularly regretted that none of his pictures were in the Tate. He was already eighty-six when we held a retrospective exhibition in Grafton Street covering paintings from 1922 to 1973. In the 1920s he had painted in France, in the 1940s and 1950s he worked in Spain and Portugal and in the 1960s he had fallen in love with Cyprus and Turkey. He also

John Nash CBE RA *Sheep in Field* c.1950 oil on canvas 45 x 35 cm 18 x 14 in

Cedric Morris *The Butcher Birds* 1940 oil on canvas 61.25 x 72.5 cm 24½ x 29 in

painted flowers and English landscapes. The show was not a great financial success as we only sold about ten pictures, however shortly before his death seven years later, I wrote to Alan Bowness at the Tate suggesting that Morris should be represented in the museum. As a result they bought three works, including a portrait of Lucian Freud, and Cedric was delighted. After his death the Tate gave him a memorial exhibition. Maggie Hambling painted a death portrait of Cedric which I considered outstanding, particularly the painting of the hands.

Richard Morphet also bought an early self-portrait by **Gilbert Spencer** for the Tate. Gilbert was a good painter but, like John Nash, he was always overshadowed by his famous brother. He lived at Walsham-le-Willows in Suffolk and benefited from the support of the Martineau family, who were also patrons of Stanley Spencer. When Gilbert's wife died, Martineau, who had been chairman of Whitbreads, rented him a cottage on his estate. He would lunch every day with them and Mrs Martineau would help him with his autobiography, which was eventually published by Chatto and Windus. Gilbert Spencer's solicitor suggested that I should go down to see him, and although I met him quite late in his life, in the 1970s, I found him very amusing. He had stopped painting by then, but had a shed containing at least ten paintings including a large work called *The Miller*. I had it cleaned and framed and we sold it for £3000, a good price in those days. When I sent him the money he told me it was 'Nice to have a few coins to chink in my pocket'.

Gilbert Spencer *The Cow Shed* c.1955 oil on canvas 45 x 35 cm 18 x 14 in

Henry Lamb *Portrait of Charlie Gallagher* 1913 49.5 x 37.5 cm 19¾ x 15 in

I see him as an important English landscape painter. His work was comparatively unknown but we did show his pictures in mixed exhibitions, although we never had enough work to mount a solo show. His reputation has suffered but the Fine Art Society has helped put him back on the map. Through Gilbert, I met Stanley Spencer on a number of occasions and sometimes showed his small oils in the gallery.

I have always admired the work of Anthony Eyton and was pleased when he had a one-man show with us in 1973, and although he moved on to another gallery, we have remained friends. One day he telephoned me saying that there was a student who might interest me. This was Alan Dodd, whose work was very skilled and slightly surrealist. He had three very successful shows with us but later turned to mural painting, where he has established a great reputation.

I never actually met **Keith Vaughan** whose main gallery was Roland Browse and Delbanco; they later passed his estate to Agnews. They offered me the pick of the estate and we were able to hold two excellent shows of his work in 1985 and 1987. I consider him to be one of the most interesting of post-war British painters, and I admire both his paintings and his drawings. His reputation has grown steadily over recent years.

One of my most important painters was **Henry Lamb**, a contemporary of Augustus John and Stanley Spencer with whom he went on painting expeditions. As a young man he had studied medicine, but gave up in 1904 in order to paint. On the outbreak of war in 1914, he resumed his studies and qualified in 1916, serving in the Royal Army Medical Corps and winning the Military Cross. He served in Macedonia with Stanley Spencer.

I met him through my friends the Kennedy family whose seven sons he had painted, but by the time I started the gallery he was long since dead. I had known him for the last eight or ten years of his life and I found him a delightful man, and a very good painter particularly in his earlier days. His early drawings when he visited Gola Island, off Donegal, in 1912–13 were just as brilliant as those of Augustus John. His wife Pansy, Lord Longford's sister, let me put on two or three shows, one in Grafton Street and the others in Bond Street and Barnes. In one there was a marvellous drawing of Dorelia, Augustus John's wife – appropriately Michael Holroyd, who had written John's biography, bought it.

I borrowed a couple of Henry Lamb pictures for a exhibition from Lord Moyne, one a wonderful portrait of Evelyn Waugh painted in 1926, the year that Waugh published *Vile Bodies* aged twenty-six. On that occasion I had to drive down to Moyne's place near Andover to pick up the picture. There were torrential floods and I got there rather late to find them sitting around the table halfway through lunch in this beautiful house. The scene reminded me of a painting by Lamb that I had borrowed from the Dover Street Arts Club, which features the artist with his back to the picture and Stanley Spencer opposite gesticulating, with Lord Moyne to one side. Lamb also painted the famous portrait of Lytton Strachey which belongs to the Tate.

The author V.S. Pritchett put me in touch with Reynolds Stone, an established engraver and typographer who had studied under Morrison, typographer of *The Times*, and under Eric Gill. He was already an elderly man with a considerable reputation when he held his first show at the New Grafton in 1968, but he went on to have four more exhibitions with us. He was greatly admired as an engraver and Kenneth Clark had published an appreciation of his work. He had designed the five-pound note and was always busy on commissions, including various things for the Royal Family and, as a result, Prince Philip came to his second exhibition in Bond Street in 1972. Stone was a quiet scholarly man whose father had been a house master at Eton. He lived in a rectory near Dorchester with his wife, whom he described as 'Terror'. She was formidable, had been a mistress of Kenneth Clark and brought his name into the conversation at the drop of a hat. I went down to Dorchester and stayed with them while choosing the work. He had a large, rather wild garden which featured in many of his watercolours. He exhibited both engravings and watercolours which were quite large and freely painted: they were popular and sold well.

I suppose one of our most successful exhibitions was the eightieth birthday show of **John Piper** in 1984, when we had some large watercolours and screen prints following his big show at the Tate. I only met John Piper on one occasion and found him highly articulate, civilised and intelligent. Some days before the show we had a telephone call from Sir Edward Heath who wanted to come and see the pictures. I told him that they would be on the floor because we had only just received them and had not yet taken down the previous exhibition. 'That's all right', he said, and turned up the next day. He was interested in the pictures of the ports which he had sailed into, such as Portland Bay and Venice. I had six paintings ready facing outwards but he said he wanted to see the rest, so I had to turn them all round and let him see the whole show. He wanted the six he had chosen, but I told him that he could not buy them before the opening. He was lecturing in Florida the following week so I asked him to phone us from the States. It was a Saturday and he was off to have lunch with Macmillan for his ninetieth birthday. When I asked him how he felt about his old boss taking an Earldom he replied 'I don't answer questions like that'.

I first met **Carel Weight** in the early 1950s before he had become Professor at the Royal College. When I was at Shell he was very helpful suggesting artists to illustrate *Land* and he also came to Shell to act as judge for the annual art competition, on which occasions he always found good things to say about the pictures. He was a very kind man, keen to help his students, ex-students and friends.

In 1958 I wrote a series about contemporary portrait painters for the *Tatler* and included Carel Weight, whom I called 'The Poet of Putney':

John Piper *Sunningwell I, Oxfordshire* 1959 watercolour and mixed media 51.25 x 56.25 cm 20⅜ x 22½ in

He believes that people should be painted in a setting and he abhors the conventional or official portraits as something stilted and almost meaningless ... For instance, in one of the portraits of Miss Orovida Pissarro, she sits in her own room, her illustrations, grandfather's writing desk behind her and an etching of Camille Pissarro in the left foreground. These objects convey her links with Pissarro.

He is a portrait painter of great integrity. He thinks that the art of portraiture has perhaps never been at a lower ebb than it is today.

Carel had a most original way of seeing things, very much his own man, and I've always believed that in time he will be considered an important painter, as important as L.S. Lowry. He is an artist you either love or hate. He painted entirely from his imagination, often London street scenes with people walking, running away from something ominous or coming out of the houses. There is a sense of foreboding in many of his pictures, and we are never quite sure what exactly is going on. He was concerned with emotions such as anger, love, hate, fear and loneliness which he emphasised in the landscapes in which his dramas were acted out.

When I started the portrait gallery Peter Greenham suggested that I should have Carel on my books and I also included his work in mixed shows. The first one-man of Carel's work was in 1974. I found it easy to sell his work, not only because of its originality but also because he kept his prices low. He always wanted his friends to be able to buy his pictures but was forced to raise his prices after Bernard Jacobson put on a show of pictures he had bought in the auction houses over several years at comparatively high prices. Carel was not interested in money: he had few commitments and he had a salary from the Royal College. In those days many artists depended on art school teaching for regular income. He never painted to sell, just for himself, and this was the secret of his success. He was always a great friend of the gallery and often introduced young artists. Sometimes we showed his work with other artists whose work was also based upon the imagination, including Mick Rooney, Helen Roeder, **Gus Cummins** and Cyril Reason.

I knew Carel socially from the early 1970s onwards. He had been living with Helen Roeder since they had met at Goldsmiths, but they did not marry until a couple of years before he died. Helen had been the librarian at the Courtauld Institute and had helped Kenneth Clark with various projects. She did paint well, but she remained a rather scholarly person. Once, sitting next to Helen at a Chelsea Arts Club dinner I asked her if I could put a rather personal question to her. 'You and Carel have been together for fifty-two years: how is it that you've never got married?' 'If we got married', she replied 'I feel that Carel would start looking at other girls'. When we first met, Carel had a studio in Chelsea Old Church Street attached to the rectory. He later moved to a house in Spencer Road, Wandsworth and had a studio in Putney which he used until his death. He would take a bus to work every day. He enjoyed good food and wine, but he never entertained at home although he was generous in his support of other artists and always attended their private views. He was a very benign man who sometimes gave an impression of vagueness, although this was something of an act. He was very astute and was an effective Professor at the College. He was awarded the CBE and later I suggested to Roger de Grey that he should be awarded a knighthood, but in fact he was made a Companion of Honour. He was rather surprised and asked me whether I had sat on a committee or something. I was delighted with his CH as he fully deserved it.

Professor Carel Weight *Street Incident* c.1974
oil on board 60 x 32 cm 24 x 12¾ in

Colin Hayes *Tibetan Farm, Ladakh* 1998 oil on canvas 40 x 50 cm 16 x 20 in

Carel was broadminded and never dismissed anything simply because it was new. This was one of the reasons why he was such a good teacher. His pupils included Kitaj, Hockney and Blake as well as artists like Linda Sutton and Eileen Hogan. The Royal College had great influence at the Academy at that time with Robert Buhler, **Ruskin Spear** and Carel all as active members. He was always keen to get Royal College people elected, often lobbying members, and he helped in getting Fred Cuming, Mick Rooney and Olwyn Bowey elected. He stood for President after Monnington's death, against Hugh Casson, and lost by a couple of votes. I was very pleased that he did not get it as it would have limited his painting. Being President is almost a full-time job, and it was easier for Hugh Casson because he had an office with staff that could continue to work in his absence at the Academy. Carel's great hero was Stanley Spencer, and his work follows in the tradition of the English eccentric. He often talked about Spencer's work and considered him the greatest English painter of the century. He also admired the work of Brueghel and Bosch. He would often come to the gallery for tea, sometimes with Olwyn Bowey, and I remember that on one occasion he bought a watercolour by Christa Gaa.

The last surviving member of that famous portrait of the painting staff at the Royal College of Art by Moynihan is **Colin Hayes**, who had a retrospective exhibition with us in 1998 with paintings dating from the 1930s onwards. His Greek landscapes are full of heat and light, painted with flat areas of hot colour which react one against the other. He gives the appearance of a reticent man, but the manner shrouds a talented and colourful painter with a steely core. His twentieth-century hero is Matisse; like the French master his paintings glow with a colourful exuberance. He read history at Oxford just before the war, although he spent much of his time at the Ruskin School of Art. On his return from the war in 1945 he met Rodrigo Moynihan, who was to become a close friend and colleague. At this time he also met Peter Greenham who was then teaching at the City Art School in Oxford, and he admits to learning much from him. In 1945 Robin Darwin appointed Moynihan as Professor of Painting at the Royal College and Moynihan in turn invited Colin to join him. Hayes became a leading member of that redoubtable painting staff from 1949 to 1984. He was very much an *éminence grise*, right-hand man first to Moynihan, then to Carel Weight. Later he was to fulfil a similar function as unofficial second in command to Sir Roger de Grey at the City and Guilds Art School. **Robert Buhler** wrote of Colin's work 'He grasps the whole and extracts the kernel in a beautifully ordered statement. To possess a painting by Colin Hayes is to own a well crafted object with a deep poetic meaning.'

Another artist closely associated with Carel Weight is Olwyn Bowey, who used to produce work for me when I was at Shell. She has developed a very personal way of painting. She often paints greenhouses with strong angles and a great sense of space and perspective.

Derek Hill was similar to Carel Weight in his generosity towards other artists. I got to know Derek very well over the years and visited him in his lovely Georgian house in Donegal, on one occasion meeting Cecil Beaton who was also a guest. My ex-wife Geraldine was in PR and was hired by Derek to get publicity for his work. He seemed to know everybody, including dukes and duchesses, and was really a social animal. I did not like all his work although some of his portraits are excellent. Through Derek Hill, I met Mary Kessell who showed with us in the early years. She was married to the designer Tom Eckersley and was one of the war artists who visited Belsen.

I was introduced to John O'Connor by Carel Weight. When we met he was Head of Colchester School of Art, a post which he held from 1948 to 1964: he now lives in Kirkcudbright. He was a close friend of John Nash and persuaded him to teach at Colchester. He paints slightly abstracted landscapes, both in oils and watercolours, which I prefer as they seem to catch the mood of the landscape so well. His East Anglian landscapes have a sense of mystery combined with good colour and spontaneity. He is also a fine draughtsman and engraver and I introduced him to Richard Ingrams, who employed him to do drawings for *The Oldie*. He has written and illustrated a number of books about the countryside and about wood engraving.

Practically my last show in Grafton Street in 1976 is worth a mention. It was by **Sir John Verney** – a most wonderful man – and consisted of his paintings and painted furniture. He had an extraordinary

Sir John Verney *Duplicity* 1982 oil on board 30 x 20 cm 12 x 8 in

sense of humour, and the furniture had scenes of nudes running about in the garden, playing croquet and that sort of thing. In fact we had both been prisoners of war in the same camp in Italy for a few months. He was really a Renaissance man: as well as painting he wrote several books. One, *A Dinner of Herbs*, was about being a prisoner of war – people used to go around the camp finding dandelion leaves and other herbs to eat – another was called *Going to the Wars*. He also produced an annual calendar for Collins called *Dodopad* with different drawings for every day, as well as a highly successful children's magazine, *The Young Elizabethan*. He was also actively involved in turning an old maltings in Farnham into an arts centre for exhibitions and concerts. He and his wife Jan later moved to Clare in Suffolk where Jan ran an antique shop. They had many interesting friends including artists such as Julian Trevelyan, Mary Fedden and Edward Ardizzone, and their house was full of paintings.

Mary Fedden and her husband Julian Trevelyan first came to the New Grafton while we were in Bond Street. Both Mary and Julian taught at the Royal College and were friends of Carel Weight. They were both with the Redfern, but I was pleased to take them on. Mary had her first solo with us in 1975 followed by others, usually two years apart. The last was in 1988 when she decided not to have any more, but she has continued to take part in group exhibitions. Over the years she has become a very good friend. Mary's work was very cheap in those days; you could buy a watercolour for £50. She has never been money minded and the incredible popularity and success of her work has really been thrust upon her. She is surprised by the huge prices her pictures go for in the salerooms. Our clients very quickly fell for her paintings and as we have a policy of not selling before the opening, we would find a queue of about twenty people waiting when we opened at 10 o'clock. Because of the demand we decided to instigate an allowance of no more than three pictures each. At one exhibition a man bought three pictures as we opened, but my assistant Sarah did not realise that his wife was there and also bought three. He was a dealer but I let it pass. Sarah even got punched in the stomach by a frail-looking old lady who had been pushed aside in the rush to buy a Fedden. I understand the popularity of her work, which I find cheerful, joyous and life enhancing.

Julian Trevelyan was a very interesting man who had studied at Cambridge before the war and had known many of the Bloomsbury Group. He was a founder member of the English Surrealists but had turned towards naive painting after the war. A nephew of the historian G.M. Trevelyan, he was himself a rather scholarly figure: he wrote several books including one about art for young people called *The Artist and his World*. He had studied in Paris and had known Picasso and Braque. He became interested in painting industrial landscapes in the 1930s, working in the Potteries and with Mass Observation in Bolton. Later he established an artistic community in Durham Wharf by the Thames. The old warehouses and chimneys along the Thames with their derelict cranes and wharves became a recurrent theme in his work. He painted from the heart, and once wrote that his paintings were felt somewhere between the heart and the eyes and not by the mind. His first show with us was in 1977. It included thirty oils, some going back

Mary Fedden *Goats* 1983
oil on board 60 x 60 cm 24 x 24 in

Julian Trevelyan *Chiswick Eyot* 1984
oil on canvas 60 x 60 cm 24 x 24 in

66

to 1936, and he also exhibited colour etchings alongside the oils. He included pictures of India, Turkey and the Canary Isles. Julian and Mary were very well suited as a couple and highly sociable, often entertaining in their home by the Thames or going out to dinner with their many friends.

Mary and Julian introduced me to **Reg Gammon**, whom Mary had met when she was President of the Royal West of England Academy. He was an amazing character with no art school training, who had worked as an illustrator for newspapers before turning to painting. He was also a good writer and produced articles as well as a book, *A Week in the Country*, which he both wrote and illustrated. During the war he bought a farm in the Llanthog Valley in Wales where he was able to observe life on a farm in detail. When I first met him he was working mostly on paper and I encouraged him to use oils and to paint what he knew and loved in a bold manner. He later wrote 'Whatever I paint, I've done. Threshing, stooking, haymaking, ploughing, scything and a bit of poaching too.' His pictures often include people working in the fields or on the coast usually with a horse and cart, but as farming methods progressed in England, he turned to Brittany for his subjects. He was influenced by Gauguin and painted in a broad, bold style using strong colours. John Russell Taylor wrote of his 'breathtaking intensity of colour … his burning reds and acid greens'. He had six exhibitions with us including a centenary show in 1994 and retrospective in 1999, and a collection of his articles and art work was published as *One Man's Furrow*. He was 103 when he died and had lived entirely from his painting. He ascribed his longevity to goats' cheese and wine, which seemed a good combination. He had a great sense of humour and we were pleased to be asked to his one-hundredth birthday party in Somerset.

I always enjoyed the company of **Edward Ardizzone** and looked forward to his shows at the gallery. He was as amusing as his pictures suggest and I see him as a modern-day Rowlandson. He was a jolly, old world sort of character: he lived in Kent and I used to go down to choose work for the exhibitions. This was always a tremendous experience, as we had an enormous glass of sherry before lunch and two bottles of Rioja between three of us over lunch. When he had his first show with us in 1975 he stayed at the Ritz: money was not a problem as he had a steady income from publishing. He taught illustration at the Royal Academy and most of the works he showed with us were watercolours. I think his work is still very underestimated.

Ivon Hitchens has always been one of my favourite artists. I like his sense of colour and the freedom of his brushwork, but there is often no rhyme or reason in them; they just work as paintings. He showed with us in mixed exhibitions and over the years I got to know him quite well. In 1986 we mounted an important exhibition devoted solely to Ivon Hitchens and **Patrick Heron**: John Read produced a *South Bank Show* about Heron's work which coincided with the exhibition.

When I first met **Dick Lee** he was teaching in the Foundation Department at Camberwell, where he taught for thirty years, and was living in Barnes. He later moved to Fakenham in Norfolk and we used to spend

Reg Gammon *Reaping with Sickles, Brittany* 1994 oil on board 50 x 60 cm 20 x 24 in

Edward Ardizzone *Moses Crossing the Waters* c.1972 watercolour on paper 20 x 27.5 cm 8 x 11 in

weekends with him in East Anglia. He was an excellent landscape painter, steeped in the Camberwell tradition, and a very genuine artist who never relied upon tricks or gimmicks to make his pictures work. I particularly liked his low-key landscapes which were intimate and restrained, but I was less happy with the larger, semi-abstract pictures which he painted later in life.

Another artist who works in East Anglia is **Fred Dubery**, whom I met through the Royal College of Art where he taught painting to photographers and where his wife, Joanne Brogden, was Professor of Fashion. I think it was largely through their influence that I was made a member of the Senior Common Room at the College. They have become close friends and I have visited them in Stowmarket where they now live. We have held a number of exhibitions of Fred's work, and I particularly liked the pictures he painted as a result of a trip to South Africa. Duberry made superb use of perspective; there were fascinating interiors and studies of Cape Dutch architecture and vineyards around Stellenbosch.

It was Heinz Roland who suggested in 1970 that we should mount an exhibition of drawings by **Josef Herman**. Born in Poland, the son of a Jewish cobbler, Herman studied at Warsaw School of Art. Fearing the German invasion he left Warsaw in 1938 and settled in Belgium, where his work was admired by the Flemish expressionist painter Permeke. In 1940 he fled to France and then to Britain, settling in Glasgow. In 1943 he moved to London and shared an exhibition at Reid and Lefèvre with Lowry, but in 1944 he went to Wales and stayed in the mining village of Ystradgynlais with the writer David Alexander Williams, and became fascinated by the mining community. He later bought an old factory which he used as a studio.

Ivon Hitchens CBE *Evening Marshes, Essex* c.1960 oil on canvas 40 x 11.25 cm 16 x 4½ in

Dick Lee *Gillian at the Piano* 1993 oil on board 26.25 x 30 cm 10½ x 12 in

Fred Dubery *Good Morning* 1989 oil on canvas 40 x 30 cm 16 x 12 in

Josef Herman OBE *The Peasant and Donkey* 1951 oil on canvas 16.25 x 21.25 cm 6½ x 8½ in

Oliver Campion *Greek Landscape* 1974 oil on canvas 50 x 60 cm 20 x 24 in

He spent several years working amongst the miners in Wales, producing some of his best work. His social sympathies lay with the working classes, and he saw manual labour as visually expressive of a man's working role in a way that intellectual activity is not. I suspect that he saw in the manual labourer a blend of heroism, fatality and sadness which combined to suggest and inspire deep and serious feelings. He always looked back to those years in Wales as the most formative in his life. When I first met Josef he was living in Suffolk near Sudbury. In his house he had sketchbooks going back many decades, but he always remembered exactly where and when he had produced a drawing. He also had a superb collection of African sculpture which was later auctioned by Christie's. I think our exhibitions created a revival of interest in Josef's work: BBC Cardiff broadcast a programme about him and he was taken up by other galleries. He was modest, very much his own man, but he did achieve recognition, becoming an RA and being made a CBE. We mostly exhibited his drawings, watercolours and smaller oils and in 2001 we mounted a retrospective after his death in the previous year.

At one point in the 1970s Roland Browse and Delbanco were dropping some of their contemporary artists and several joined the New Grafton. We gave Zdzislaw Ruszkowski a show in 1978 which was very colourful and sold well. He had come to Scotland during the war with the Polish army and had stayed in this country. We also took on Fred Uhlman whose earlier, looser paintings I liked. **Oliver Campion** was also an excellent colourist, possibly himself influenced by the same European tradition. He lived in Holland Park but also had a house near Montpellier, and liked to paint sunlit landscapes in France and Spain. I admired the freedom of his landscapes and felt that he never achieved the recognition he deserved. I thought his portraits were outstanding. He had trained as a solicitor and only turned to painting later in life. I encouraged him to study art and he went to the Slade. He was very modest and terribly nervous before an exhibition, but he needn't have worried as they were always highly successful.

Another painter of the Mediterranean, in particular Greece and Italy, was Clothilde Peploe. She was born in Florence where her American father owned a palace and she married Willie Peploe, the son of the Scottish painter S.J. Peploe. Elisabeth Sorrell also came from a very artistic background. She was married to the artist Alan Sorrell and both her children, Richard and Julia, are successful painters. She lived in Thundersley in Essex and had a huge collection of Victorian dolls which often appeared in her watercolours. She also painted flowers and wildlife and was described by John Ward as 'one of the finest and most original watercolourists of today'.

When I first met **Ken Howard** he was a young, unknown artist doing a certain amount of commercial work, such as drawings for the telephone books, to supplement his income from painting. He worked with me on *Catalyst* when I was at Shell, having been recommended by Olwyn Bowey. Some years later the Imperial War Museum was looking for an artist to go to Northern Ireland and I was consulted on the appointment. I recommended Ken, although the final decision was made by a small committee. I think that this appointment as War Artist in Northern Ireland greatly helped Ken's career. The Museum would take twelve pictures while individual regiments also commissioned work; one of these sent him to Borneo to record their action there.

When I started the New Grafton Ken approached me for a show. He had already had a successful one in Cork Street and I gave him a one-man show in 1971; since then he has been a regular exhibitor at the gallery. In 1971 he was painting subjects such as railway sidings and City of London scenes – mostly churches – in a dark palette, but like so many painters, his palette has lightened with time. For his next show in 1974 he was moving away from London scenes towards Italy, and towards the end of the 1970s his work was becoming very popular with the public. He was also showing at the Oscar and Peter Johnson gallery, although he stayed with me when I moved to Barnes. Bernard Dunstan was his champion at the Royal Academy, supported by Carel Weight, and he was elected an Associate in 1978. It had long been his ambition to become an RA and he has been a very active member. At his most recent exhibition with us in 2000, he sold all sixty of his pictures on the first day.

I first met David Wolfers when he was working for Shell, commissioning artists to produce illustrations for the two magazines he ran. I believe it was Olwyn Bowey who suggested me, at the time a young unknown painter. I remember returning to London on a train with David when he told me that he really would like to run his own gallery rather than work for Shell. I replied, rather tactlessly, that if he really wanted to run a gallery, he would have done so by now. I did not hear from him for some time, and I thought I had upset him, but when I next met him in Bond Street, he told me that he had started the New Grafton Gallery. In fact I was with the Whibley Gallery nearby, but I was not entirely happy with their other artists. I had my first show in 1971 at the gallery in Grafton Street which was a lovely space on two levels, and I have remained with David ever since, in Bond Street and in Barnes.

David was never effusive about an artist's work; when he came to select a show his comments were usually limited to 'yes' or 'no' with a very occasional 'I rather like that'. This understatement hid a very good eye: I remember I had spent hours on a painting of Richmond Bridge for a show. David was inclined to leave it out, but because I had been so involved with the painting, I insisted on including it. The moment I walked into the gallery I realised that David had been right and that it was the weakest picture in the show. Sometimes I felt that he was genuinely unenthusiastic about my work and in 1979 I wrote to him suggesting that ... I should maybe go elsewhere. He replied immediately, saying 'You should know, Ken, that I would never show any work that I did not both respect and like'. This determination only to represent artists whom he personally respected, whether totally commercial or not, was what I really admired about David. His clients also knew that they would always find work of a consistent quality in the gallery.

David disliked flashy painting, or pictures which depended upon visual tricks, and on several occasions rejected work of mine, which I thought was loose and fluent, as being 'too clever'. He got on very well with my late wife, Christa Gaa, and they had a mutual respect and understanding. David always admired her quiet understated style and I think their personalities were well suited.

He did an enormous amount for young artists, some of whom he discovered himself at the Royal Academy Schools, some who were introduced to him by other artists. For example, I introduced him to Jacqueline Williams. Some dealers only have an eye for a good seller, whereas David had an eye for a good picture which might not necessarily be a good seller, and he was prepared to stay with artists as they developed. He never told me what to paint, he never asked for subjects that he knew he could sell: for example, he never asked for another studio interior or a Venetian view. I also liked the

Ken Howard *Model Resting, Cornwall* *c.*1998 oil on canvas 100 x 120 cm 40 x 48 in

Christa Gaa *Camellia Still Life* 1990 watercolour 31.25 x 38.75 cm 12½ x 15½ in

way he treated young artists on exactly the same terms as older established artists. He never asked for contributions towards catalogues, advertising or the private view, and he knew that some of his shows, especially of new artists, might not make any money. He promoted unknown names on the strength of his better-established artists.

I think his success lay in the fact that he stayed true to his area of British art. There has been some marvellous figurative painting in Britain since the war, far better than the equivalent in France or Italy, and the New Grafton is at the centre of modern figurative painting in England. He was a great supporter of the New English Art Club which encourages this aspect of English painting, and many NEAC artists showed with him.

Ken Howard RA NEAC RWS

I also admired the marvellous watercolours of **Christa Gaa**, Ken's wife, whose pictures had great depth of feeling and intensity. Her language is personal and instantly recognisable. Her great loves in painting were Chardin, Bonnard and Morandi; each influenced her work profoundly but it is her own spirit and language which shines through her work. Carel Weight believed that she was one of the most outstanding watercolourists of her period, and her premature death was a great loss. Bernard Dunstan wrote in her obituary in the *Independent*:

Gaa was a watercolour painter of a very individual kind who died at the height of her powers. She is perhaps best known as a painter of still-life. This is a genre with which watercolour is not usually associated nowadays.... But she used it with a quiet virtuosity, working in a low key with a rich orchestra of colour, and yet never losing the essential freshness of watercolour, or merely imitating the depth of oil.

I think it was Carel Weight who first introduced me to **Fred Cuming** and I immediately liked his work, showing some at mixed exhibitions before giving him his first one-man with us in 1985. The first time he took part in a mixed exhibition, his pictures never arrived so after that Fred put his wife, Audrey, in charge and since then there has been no problem! He had been a student at the Royal College, overlapping with Ken Howard, and he was put up for membership of the Royal Academy in the days when the Royal College staff had influence there. When I first met Fred he was living at Hythe and I went down to stay with him and see his work. I have always admired the strong element of poetry in his work, which combined with his originality makes us look at his subjects in a very different and unique way. He manages to make even the most mundane and commonplace view, such as a petrol station at night, a cinema at sunset or even a simple corner shop, seem interesting and different. It has taken many years for Fred to gain the recognition he deserves, but with the publication of his book *A Figure in the Landscape* and with a room devoted to his work at the Royal Academy Summer Show in 2001, I feel that he has finally arrived.

Fred is a very versatile painter. He can turn his hand to landscape, interiors, portraits, still lifes and nudes and works equally well in oils, watercolours and etching. He is a natural painter who never appears to have to struggle for effect. His landscapes are very much in the English tradition and his marvellous studies of clouds can be compared to Constable. His obsession with Camber Sands I see as a parallel to Cézanne's fascination with Mont Ste Victoire. He is also a great reader with many interests in literature, music and art. Fred and Audrey have become close friends and we often go down to stay with them in their house near Rye in Kent. We try to go on a trip for three nights each year visiting various parts of the country such as Devon or Oxfordshire. Fred does some work, always taking a sketchbook with him, and we also make a point of visiting some interesting collections of paintings.

> *It was Carel Weight who first told me about David Wolfers and his gallery in the West End. I invited David down to Folkestone in 1972 to see my exhibition at the New Metropole Gallery, but I did not then know the effect that he was to have on my life. At that time I was in a particularly unstable stage of development, experimenting with various styles and theories. David and his wife stayed with us in Hythe overnight and he was encouraging about my work, beginning to show my paintings in his gallery.*

> *A very particular man, exact and precise, I think he was a little confused by my chaotic approach to painting. He liked to know exactly what he was getting for an exhibition, something I could not always clearly state. When he first started coming to the studio before an exhibition, he would like to see the finished work and know the titles and sizes for the catalogue. Over the years I managed to change all that, and he began to understand my way (I hesitate to say method) of working. Eventually we got to the stage where half the pictures would be completed, the rest in various degrees of finish, some barely started. He would raise his eyes to the heavens, while I would give him measurements, always height first, and then the titles. This procedure would continue amidst gales of laughter as we searched for suitable titles.*

> *Out of a purely business association, there developed a deep friendship and understanding. I trusted David implicitly; his word was his bond and he helped me and my family through some difficult times. His guidance to me as an artist was invaluable. I discovered that, behind his façade, he was not serious. He loved to play practical jokes such as disguising his voice on the telephone to catch me out. He also loved sport and was an extremely good tennis player. I played him at singles once, and only once, as he ran me around the court until I was exhausted. I felt so ill that I went to hospital for a check up and after that we only played doubles. He was also a keen cricket player.*

Fred Cuming RA *Dawn Sea* 2000 oil on canvas 90 x 90 cm 36 x 36 in

Tom Coates *Behind the Uffizi, Florence* 1998 oil on canvas 100 x 75 cm 40 x 30 in

On his visits to us we would go out to good restaurants, as he loved food, wine and company. He was always a generous host. After a good meal there was nothing he liked better than to watch a movie, the Marx Brothers, Chaplin, Buster Keaton, Laurel and Hardy being amongst his favourites. I have a collection of these films and he always asked to see them. David also read a great deal and, with an extraordinary memory, he was very knowledgeable about literature.

David and Jacqueline often accompanied us in 'jaunts' to several parts of the country. These included visits to the Lake District, Norfolk, Yorkshire, Oxford, Cambridge and Dorset, where in Puddletown he was delighted to find for my wife a copy of the Shell Guide to Dorset *which Paul Nash had illustrated and David had edited. We also went to France together, visiting Monet's Garden at Giverny, Honfleur and Paris. His knowledge of art history was encyclopaedic and we would visit collections, cathedrals, gardens, always followed by a good meal. Our last 'jaunt' just before Christmas 2001 was to David's beloved Oxford. We visited the Ashmolean and Worcester College, which he knew intimately from his student days.*

The New Grafton Gallery became one of the most respected and successful in London, but it was a reflection of the man. Always kind, David looked after his staff and his artists. Once he had accepted an artist he remained faithful to that artist and in return demanded loyalty from them.

Fred Cuming RA NEAC

Tom Coates had his first show with us in 1988 and has shown regularly with us ever since. He is an artist in the New English tradition, influenced by painters such as Sickert and Greenham, and has a wide range of subjects and techniques. He works equally confidently in oils, pastels and watercolour and paints landscapes, portraits, nudes, and interiors, but it is the intensity and sensitivity of his landscapes which I particularly like. I admire the way he portrays Venice in winter light rather than in the full sunlight of summer so favoured by most artists. Tom often manages to capture a familiar subject from a different angle or point of view. He is a vigorous and spontaneous painter who reacts with a sense of immediacy to what he sees. He is also a master draughtsman, a rare talent in today's world. Tom is also a great collector of pictures; I feel that we have something there in common, and I always enjoy his company.

I first met David during the 1960s when I was a student at the Royal Academy Schools. I was encouraged to look at commercial galleries, including the Fine Art Society and the New Grafton, by Charles Mahoney and by Peter Greenham, who was then a visiting lecturer at the Schools. It was marvellous to see paintings by those artists I particularly admired, Greenham, Weight and Ruskin

Spear. I think I was at first rather frightened of David and it took some time to come to understand him.

When the New Grafton moved to Barnes I used to visit to see exhibitions and I was always amazed by the quality and variety of the stock that the gallery held. Being a figurative painter, who was at that time finding his way, it was important to see what was going on. Over the years I bought many pictures from the gallery including works by Greenham, Lee, Howard, Cuming, Weight, Fedden and Duberry. I even remember queuing outside for one show and getting the famous raffle ticket.

I took part in a mixed exhibition before being invited to have a one-man show in 1988, since then I have had regular one-man exhibitions and I feel that I have learnt something from each. David always had an eye for both a good picture and a good seller. When I was planning my second one-man I was contemplating going to Egypt to follow in the footsteps of David Roberts, but when I told David about my plan, he put his arm round my shoulders and said quietly 'Venice is still a good seller'. My trip to Egypt had to wait for another occasion. David never dictated the subject for an exhibition and his advice was always useful, especially about presentation of pictures. He was always encouraging about my work, but never effusive in his praise. He once said 'You're improving: in twenty years you'll have a sell out'. He was a very straightforward and fair dealer who kept his commission reasonable and was never greedy, but in return he demanded loyalty from his artists. For me the New Grafton has been very much part of my life.

We used to meet through the New English Art Club where David was a patron and keen supporter. He helped in many ways, not least by exhibiting many NEAC members' work. We also met socially, and Mary and I would often stay with David and Jacqueline in London. He was always very generous and loved eating out. He also had a great sense of mischievous fun which often involved playing ball games. One evening at the Garrick Club we were sitting at the long table when all the other members had gone, and David insisted on playing cricket on the table using fruit for the ball and the menu card for the bat. I bowled and he knocked me all round the room. He was rather surprised when Mary clean bowled him!

My last show at the New Grafton was in November 2001 and was his last one-man exhibition. When I came to the gallery shortly before Christmas to collect the cheque, David disappeared into the back room and returned with a Peter Greenham portrait of an elderly lady in a grey dress. It is a superb portrait with shimmering silvery tones and quite large. He simply said 'You have collected many pictures over the years and I want you to have this'. He knew that I had always wanted a Greenham portrait, but I was so surprised that I did not really thank him enough. Sadly I never had the opportunity to thank him properly.

Tom Coates NEAC RP RBA PPS

84

Edmund Fairfax-Lucy *The Stable Roof at Charlecote, January 1976* 1976 oil on board 35 x 50 cm 14 x 20 in

Another artist whose talent I greatly admire is **Edmund Fairfax-Lucy**, who was a student under Peter Greenham at the Royal Academy Schools. He shares Peter's sensitive approach to painting, searching rather than stating, but he sometimes finds it difficult to finish a picture. A couple of weeks before his first show with us in Bond Street in 1975 he rang up to say that he did not have enough pictures; luckily Colin Hayes and Maurice Sheppard were able to stand in to make it a three-man show. We never quite knew what was coming in for an exhibition, and sometimes he would take away work which he considered unsuitable. His work is free, delicate and almost visionary in its intensity.

Richard Pikesley, another student of Peter Greenham, is someone whose work has progressed enormously in recent years. He has an extraordinary feel for landscape, in particular the West Country, and he paints water extremely well. The sense of light in his pictures is marvellous and I admire his sea and river views: his pictures of Weymouth have a real sparkle. He is an artist who is developing and I have great confidence in him.

I first became aware of the New Grafton when I was a foundation student at Harrow School of Art. I was lucky enough to have Ken Howard as a tutor and when he had his first show at the gallery in Grafton Street I went along. I liked the kind of work that the gallery was showing and I returned on a regular basis. There was a thread of a particular sensibility which runs through all the shows at the gallery which appeals to me. After Harrow I went to Canterbury School of Art where I found it difficult to study. There were only two kinds of painting on offer, Surrealism or Abstraction, which were not my interest, so I often returned to the New Grafton to see the kind of painting which did interest me. The Peter Greenham exhibitions were a revelation and I felt I was seeing the sort of pictures that I would like to paint. So the New Grafton has been an important part of my art education.

After a short period teaching, I decided to concentrate on painting, and I went to see Ken Howard in Mousehole with some of my pictures. He selected three little paintings which he took to his framer and then showed them to David. Like many other artists, I started to show in the annual mixed exhibitions, 'Smaller Pictures for Christmas and New Year' and 'Artists of Today and Tomorrow', progressing towards a two-man show followed by a one-man.

When David came to my studio to choose work for an exhibition, he would take off his shoes and put on a pair of slippers. He would test me by asking me for lists of my favourite painters. I shared his admiration for Piero della Francesca but never quite got Uccello. I loved Giovanni Bellini, who I don't think was on David's 'A' list, and all the English outsiders he loved so much. My list would always include William Blake, Samuel Palmer, Stanley Spencer and Paul Nash, none of whom were part of the English mainstream, let alone the European.

My first one-man show in 1991 was not an enormous success. I had rather too many small pictures but despite mediocre sales, which probably only just broke even for the gallery, I was invited back for another. Since then every show has done better than the previous one, and whereas many dealers would not have invited me back for a second one-man, David had confidence in my work. Over the years the New Grafton has helped many young artists on their way, giving them exposure and taking a financial risk. David knew that it takes time for an artist to become a good seller, and he was prepared to wait.

For a solo show David would like to see all the paintings and settle the catalogue well in advance. At first I found this difficult as it brought my painting deadline forward by about six weeks. Later I

Richard Pikesley *Crowds on the Riva degli Schiavoni* 1995 oil on canvas 75 x 90 cm 30 x 36 in

Peter Kuhfeld *Kathryn Reading* 1989 oil on canvas 35 x 50 cm 14 x 20 in

Martin Yeoman *Rainy Day, Venice* 2000 oil on paper 20 x 25 cm 8 x 10 in

realised that it stopped me panicking right up to the last minute. It's not unknown for a painter to deliver paintings still wet for an exhibition, racked with doubt as to how to resolve a troublesome passage. At first David would puzzle me with his lack of comment about each picture, but in time I came to value the fact that he didn't suggest alterations or even talk about what he did like in a particular painting.

I respected David's artistic judgement and taste. When he was selecting pictures he never asked you to change them or even discussed their merits or faults. He hated anything flashy or meretricious. Pictures were either in or out. He did not judge a picture on its saleability, but on the basis of what he considered to be good and original. He liked a particularly English, as opposed to Scottish, way of painting: a rather quiet, understated, painterly approach, although he also had a wider range of taste, such as the more eccentric approach of Carel Weight and his circle, and the colourful style of some of his younger painters.

David has been a great help to me, boosting my confidence over the years, and in return I have a loyalty to the gallery. I have been asked to show elsewhere, but I am comfortable at the New Grafton. The gallery never feels like a commercial venture, but more like an interesting and personal collection of pictures. This atmosphere inspires confidence amongst the clients, who realise that David has made a careful and individual selection. The prices are also kept reasonable. I have seen many artists who have been flattered by galleries to push up their prices only to find that they cannot be sustained. David has always been very realistic about pricing.

Richard Pikesley NEAC

Two other artists influenced by Peter Greenham at the Schools have shown with me in the past: **Peter Kuhfeld**, and **Martin Yeoman** who is an exceptional draughtsman. I particularly admired the self portrait that Martin did in silver point which is in Dudley Dodd's collection. Both Sir Brinsley Ford and Dudley Dodd respected the work of Cherryl Fountain, another RA Schools student, and they came down to Barnes for the opening of her show in 1986. I liked the quirkiness of her work, and her attention to detail which never became overworked or dull. **Christopher Hall** is also individual and detailed, but never sentimental or sweet. His naive paintings of France and Italy are popular, in particular his marvellous pictures of lavender in flower.

I first saw the work of **Ruth Stage** at the Schools and was very impressed. She was already working in tempera having been inspired by Jane Dowling and I believe that she has a very original way of seeing landscape, and is particularly good at painting water and its effects. She has an extraordinary sense of

Christopher Hall *Catley Lane Head, Rooley Moor* (*Lancashire*) 1995 oil on board 27.5 x 21.25 cm 11 x 8½ in

Ruth Stage *Evening Stroll, Byron Bay* 2001 egg tempera 50 x 57.5 cm 20 x 23 in

pattern which, combined with marvellous colour, results in very original and individual works. Her technique is unusual which adds to the particular quality of her work, and she deserved to be elected to the New English Art Club. I put her in for the Villiers David Prize for artists under thirty-five and she won second prize for two years. I am still hoping that she will win outright. Ruth took part in a recent exhibition we held of the newly formed Egg Tempera Society of which Mick Rooney is President.

We have shown **Mick Rooney**'s work in several two or three man exhibitions, but in 2003 he is having his first solo with us. He is an artist with great imagination and a strong sense of pattern and colour, somewhat in the tradition of Carel Weight and even Stanley Spencer. He was introduced to us by Carel when he was teaching at the Royal Academy Schools and they share a great sense of fun. I believe that his work will come to be more widely recognised than it is at present.

I met David Wolfers through Carel and I have taken part in two four man shows, in 1990 with Carel Weight, Colin Hayes, Olwyn Bowey and in 1993 with Carel, Cyril Reason, and Helen Roeder.... These group shows in Barnes did not appear like commercial exhibitions, but rather as celebrations of the art of Carel and his friends.

I admired the way David was interested in unusual painters who were not maybe mainstream, for example Cyril Reason and Joseph Herman. Over his many years as a gallery owner David built up a huge knowledge about post-war English artists and was often involved in the estates of artists he has shown. I appreciated his broad range of interest from Peter Greenham, who I think helped form his taste, to the drawings of Elisabeth Frink which many people at the time thought provocative and even aggressive. He always took a great interest in drawing, and directed his clients towards the graphic work of artists like Frink, Herman, Lamb, Piper and Nash. He really dug and delved into twentieth-century British drawing.

I think that David will be regarded as an important dealer, rather like Vollard or Theo Van Gogh, and like them he was very much hands-on. He was always behind his desk in Barnes and was very much an involved and active gallery owner. This inspired confidence in his artists and his clients. I often passed by the gallery in the No.9 bus and when I saw David at his desk, I knew all was well in the art world!

When I was in charge of painting at the Royal Academy Schools I saw the interest that David took in young artists: he certainly helped Ruth Stage, Sarah Spencer and Jacqueline Williams on their way. More recently when the reformed Egg Tempera Society held an exhibition at Leighton House, David came along and selected six artists for an egg tempera exhibition at the New Grafton. He always stuck to his guns, and followed his own road. He knew the sort of art that appealed to him

Mick Rooney RA *Moving Day* 1992 oil on canvas 60 x 80 cm 24 x 32 in

and was not diverted from it by the hope of great wealth. His gallery covered the middle ground in English art, always with a touch of poetry, and if you want to see this kind of art, you have to go to Barnes.

Mick Rooney RA NEAC

Sarah Spencer was also a 'find' at the RA Schools. Her work is very poetic and charming, but she is a slow, careful worker, more so since she became a mother and involved in family life. I admire the intensity of her work with its muted tones and quiet colours; the paintings have great presence and power despite being quite small. I also discovered Jacqueline Williams and **Julian Bailey** at an Academy Schools exhibition. Julian uses very expressive brushwork, possibly influenced by Nicholas de Stael and Auerbach, but his work remains figurative and highly individual. I feel that he is developing into a significant painter. His figures are strong, even monumental, and painted with great gusto, as can be seen in his series of pub interiors. I have enjoyed seeing his work develop and always look forward to visiting him and his family in Dorset. Although he does not like one-man shows, his work sells very well and people appreciate his painterly approach.

I felt that the work of **Jacqueline Williams** was far ahead of her years when I first saw it at the Royal Academy Schools and I invited her to show with us. Her first solo exhibition in 1989 was a huge success and included a series of very large interiors with still life on checked tablecloths, sometimes with a self-portrait. They were very impressive and intense.

I have only recently met **Peter Brook**, but I have enjoyed showing his work at the New Grafton where he had his first one-man show in 1999. He is a delightful eccentric Yorkshireman, a friend of Lowry and Craigie Aitchison, and likes many of the same artists that I do. For a number of years he had been buying Carel Weights and Reg Gammons from the New Grafton through the actress Polly James, and when Polly brought in a book by Peter, I decided to go up to Yorkshire to see him. He is a Yorkshireman from the tip of his toes to the top of his head. The craggy winter landscape he portrays in his paintings reflects the lie of the land where he lives. Cézanne painted Mount Ste Victoire almost endlessly: Peter is equally in love with the Pennines of West Yorkshire. The strong feelings which emerge give his work a personal quality, one which has attracted diverse collectors over the years, many of them from the acting profession. The late James Mason had over thirty of his paintings, likewise Tom Courtney is a great enthusiast. We had an interesting time with Peter, his wife Molly, and Shep the dog. I particularly like his paintings with cold sunsets, red skies and snow which capture the essence of the bleak Northern winter landscape.

Sarah Spencer *St Ives Harbour* 1996 oil on board 13.75 x 18.75 cm 5½ x 7½ in

Julian Bailey *Four People at a Table* 2000 oil on board 45 x 50 cm 18 x 20 in

Jacqueline Williams *Still Life with Red Lamp* 1994 oil on canvas 75 x 90 cm 30 x 36 in

Peter Brook *Having a Few Words with the Donkey* 1999
oil on board 45 x 50 in 18 x 20 in

Another artist who loved the Northern landscape was **Sheila Fell**, whose work was developing when she died aged forty-eight. She was born in Cumberland and loved to paint semi-industrial landscapes in Cumbria. Lowry had noticed her work and she was taken up by Helen Lessore. When she came to us in 1979 she had not had a London show for fifteen years. Tragically she had a fall in her studio while the exhibition was on and died as a result.

Alex Lumley produces unusual landscapes and seascapes, often in mixed media. They are on a modest scale but have considerable impact. **Anthea Craigmyle** is more of a naive painter. She attended Chelsea School of Art in the early 1950s where her tutors were Ceri Richards and Julian Trevelyan. A friend of Mary Fedden, she used to have a studio in Chiswick, but now spends most of her time in the Scottish Highlands. Her painting is a mixture of the real and the fantasy world. The paintings of Susan-Jayne Hocking and **Pip Todd Warmoth**, both of whom studied at the Royal Academy Schools, are based on their travels abroad and both have established a following.

In recent years I have been discovering interesting artists at the City and Guilds School of Art, where drawing is still important. **Alison Sloga** studied there and has had some successful shows with us. She is

Sheila Fell *Welsh Farmyard* 1979 oil on canvas 60 x 90 cm 24 x 36 in

a visionary painter whose work is quite different and unique, powerful and yet reflective. She did a series based on war memorials and another on Battersea Power Station. She has done a series of paintings of eggs, either single or in pairs, which are pictures for meditation. **Alasdair Rennie** also trained at the City and Guilds where he won the David Wolfers Travelling Scholarship. I like his bleak Norfolk landscapes, his large beach scenes with great skies and also his Scottish landscapes. The third artist from the City and Guilds was **Mark Adlington**, a remarkable painter of animals.

I first came across the New Grafton in 1985. I was an almost completely inexperienced collector having bought only one picture up to that time, a pen and ink drawing by Adrian Daintry. David was open and welcoming; he played an important role in both giving me the confidence to buy a picture that I liked, and in educating me in figurative Modern British Art. I never felt that I had been 'sold' a picture; it was more as if I was being guided to something that suited my taste. He did not try to sell, rather he found out what sort of pictures I liked and pointed me towards those artists whom he thought I might find interesting. This approach was in harsh contrast to the art scene that I was to experience later in New York, and was, I feel, fundamental to the success of the gallery.

Alex Lumley *Huts, Zandfoort* 2001 mixed media 28.75 x 37.5 cm 11½ x 15 in

Over the years I bought a number of pictures by artists showing at the gallery including Elisabeth Frink, Fred Cuming, Mary Fedden, John Nash, Edward Fairfax-Lucy and Tom Coates. As well as showing these well established painters, David had a reputation for exhibiting the work of younger artists which made repeat visits to the gallery interesting. It was his belief in these younger painters that inspired confidence in his customers. David made Modern British Art accessible to me and started me on what has been a most enjoyable road as a collector. His passion for art came through to those lucky enough to know him and he inspired me, amongst many other collectors.

Tyrrell Young

I first met David in 1968 when the New Grafton Gallery opened, as my father was one of the original backers. It was a lovely gallery with a split level where eighteenth- and nineteenth-century artists were exhibited along with living painters below. My father bought a number of pictures from the gallery including works by Carel Weight, Frink, Elliott Hodgkin, Alan Dodd and Orovida Pissarro. Over the years I met David when he stayed with my parents in Suffolk. He was always a quiet and dignified man full of hidden depths.

It was only in 1991 when we really got to know each other that my eyes were opened to the Modern British movement which he so loved. We would go to the degree shows together where he would spot young painters at the Royal Academy Schools and the City and Guilds School of Art. He was extremely encouraging to the young artists whose work he liked, often eventually giving them their own shows. These included Pip Todd Warmoth, Mark Adlington, Alasdair Rennie, Ruth Stage, Julian Bailey and Sue Hocking. David was immensely loyal to his painters and this they really appreciated. He was proud of them when they did well although he often said very little.

He loved the work of Peter Greenham's pupils, Edmund Fairfax-Lucy, Martin Yeoman, Anne Shrager and Peter Kuhfeld and of Ken Howard, Fred Cuming, Richard Pikesley and Mick Rooney. His mixed shows were a feast for the eye, with pictures ranging from John Nash to Freddie Gore and Colin Hayes as well as his regular exhibitors. He was succinct in his praise for his artists, which they often found daunting – 'Yes' was praise indeed. Quite often they would telephone me to ask if David liked their work, as it was only at home that he would quietly say that he thought their work was very good indeed: so at least I could assure them that he loved it.

The figure of him sitting every day at his desk in the window in the gallery at Barnes was reassuring to both client and artist. The gallery had an atmosphere of calm, although an enormous amount of organisation continued in the background for each exhibition; addressing and filling envelopes and reassuring the nervous artist whose show was the next in line. David weathered the storms of the art world in the late 1980s and early 1990s by continuing to exhibit those he believed in and not going in for the installation artists who were so fashionable at the time.

He advised many people on the first items for their collection and from his solid and knowing eye they learnt to look at pictures and continued to build. So many people have told me that David started them on the road of appreciating and collecting pictures. David and the New Grafton were as one, his abiding interest and passion. Even on holiday he wanted to know what was happening and he hated to be away from the gallery for too long.

Jacqueline Wolfers

Alison Sloga *Fragments Driver 2* 2000 oil on canvas 75 x 75 cm 30 x 30 in

Conclusion

The New Grafton Gallery is a phenomenon in British post-war art: a small independent gallery situated outside the West End which attracted many of the leading figurative artists of the period. It has a reputation which some galleries envy, even though many of its artists could have achieved West End prices in more aggressive galleries. Its name and following amongst both artists and buyers is due entirely to David Wolfers' single-minded pursuit of his dream – a gallery in which quality and personal rapport are more important than financial considerations.

To many, David was a man of few words – rarely effusive, even about work which he admired, and there were periods when the shy and reticent aspect of his character dominated. At other times, especially in the company of artists who were often friends, he would become extrovert and playful, an aspect of his character that was reflected in his love of bright ties and blazers. His exploits at indoor cricket at the Garrick Club have been recorded, as has his prowess at tennis with Fred Cuming. When Julian Bailey got married in Burford, Oxfordshire, David attended and afterwards organised an ad hoc cricket match: already in his seventies, he outplayed and outran many younger players.

At the 1981 Bath Festival, David became infuriated by a dealer who had given Princess Margaret a picture in a manner which he thought was a crude publicity stunt. The next day he organised his own form of publicity, arriving at the exhibition hall with a pair of handcuffs he had bought in an antique shop and handcuffing himself to an Elisabeth Frink statue by the entrance. The plan was certainly effective and annoyed a good number of dealers, but backfired when he realised that there were no keys to the handcuffs. Eventually the fire brigade was called to cut him free!

David had a need for routine. He worked every day in the gallery, taking a break after lunch at home to rest or watch cricket on television. He liked to eat in restaurants he knew, and his clubs – the Arts Club, the Colony Room and above all the Garrick – played an important part in his routine. He enjoyed travelling, but tended to return to the same places and eat in the same restaurants. Italy, especially Sicily and Venice, was a great favourite, but he also loved Greece, in particular Crete where he struck up a friendship with a local taxi driver. France remained dear to David, and he returned regularly to the Northern French ports, Paris and the South. He spoke good French and was embarking upon learning Italian when he died. In England, he particularly liked Oxford and would find any excuse to revisit the haunts of his student days. He would call in at his old college, eat at The Randolph and order new trousers from Hall Brothers, the tailors. He had a great passion for the theatre which went back to his Oxford days. One of his sergeants from the war days worked in the National Theatre and David would take every opportunity to see new productions. He read poetry and always looked for poetry and individuality in pictures, believing that man's inner life was about poetry.

David Wolfers was passionate about English painting of the twentieth century and believed that a figurative tradition had been established which could rival any Continental school. On his travels to Europe it was inevitable that he compared contemporary painting in those countries to what he saw in Britain. He felt that the expectations of the art world and the weight of artistic tradition had led to a decline in work both from the School of Paris and contemporary Italian artists. He was constantly disappointed by what he saw in commercial galleries and lamented the loss of a great tradition.

David did not favour a particular style of painting, although his interest lay solely in representational work, and the choices he made were often surprising. His taste was eclectic, but was always centred upon work which displayed honesty and commitment. He admired painting which was genuine and had not been created solely in order to sell. While he used to say that he derived great pleasure from sending cheques to artists after exhibitions, he was always wary of those whose main objective was to maximise sales and profits. At times his dislike of commercialism put him at odds with artists and he was distrustful of those whose success had rendered them overconfident. 'He's become rather grand, you know', was a comment he made on several occasions.

David enjoyed the company of genuine artists whose life revolved around their paintings, and he appreciated the unworldly quality of men such as Carel Weight, Reg Gammon, Gilbert Spencer and John Nash. He had a great regard for the eccentric streak which runs through English painting from Blake and Samuel Palmer to Carel Weight, Edward Burra, and the brothers Stanley and Gilbert Spencer. He found pictures with a story fascinating, and rejected Whistler's contention that narrative art was old fashioned. Carel Weight's depiction of the streets of London, in which both sinister and amusing events are taking place, appealed to David, who was always more at home in London than in the country. He enjoyed Weight's sense of humour and saw in his work a direct link with Stanley Spencer and the English eccentric tradition.

The concept of the English countryman in art greatly appealed to David, who enjoyed trips into the countryside visiting artists' studios. He remembered his East Anglian trips to John Nash, John Aldridge,

John O'Connor, Cedric Morris and Fred Dubery with pleasure, while Reg Gammon and Reynolds Stone appealed to his idea of how an artist should approach the landscape. He often said that he felt uncomfortable in the country and much preferred being in London or Paris, but he loved to listen to John Nash, Reg Gammon and more recently Peter Brook who all had a deep understanding and knowledge of the ways of the country. He liked the fact that these artists were removed from London and the art world, and were not looking over their shoulders at what was going on in Burlington House or Bond Street. This quality of detachment is evident in the work of Nash, Gammon and Aldridge, and it may be this sincerity, even humility, which attracted him. Gilbert Spencer's autobiography was one of his favourite books, because he admired Spencer's honesty and the simplicity of his writing.

A totally different tradition in English painting came through the influence of Sickert and the Camden Town School. Influenced by French Impressionism and in particular by the work of Degas, Sickert developed a powerful tonal approach to interiors, figures and landscapes. His influence on the Camden Town Group was vital as artists such as Ginner, Gore, Lucien Pissarro and Gilman developed a style which links Impressionist brushwork and composition with an English tonality, understatement and subject matter. Artists such as Peter Greenham and Ruskin Spear carried this tradition into the post-war period, and its influence is still felt today in the work of Tom Coates, Ken Howard, Edmund Fairfax-Lucy and Fred Cuming. The understated qualities of the Camden Town artists appealed to the more reticent side of David's character – he always admired work which suggested rather than stated.

Many years ago, David started visiting the Royal Academy schools exhibitions often with Peter Greenham, and he began to take a great interest in the development of young artists. He liked to be something of a mentor, helping an artist to develop and suggesting possible ideas, and became involved with the City and Guilds School when it was under Roger de Grey. Many of his more recent successes – notably Ruth Stage, Mark Adlington, Alasdair Rennie and Alison Sloga – came from there, and all of them benefited from the David Wolfers Travelling scholarship which helped provide funds for foreign travel. He was also involved with the Wolfers-O'Neill Foundation, which his daughter Claudia established with Francis O'Neill to provide funds for artists in mid-career to take time out and develop.

The independence of those painters who had deliberately ploughed their own furrow has a parallel in the history of the New Grafton. David was fiercely independent, refusing to have any partners or long term investors, and insisting upon repaying his original investors as soon as possible. He was extremely careful with the limited funds at his disposal. Unlike many gallery owners, he refused offers of financial involvement and treasured his self-reliance. When the gallery moved to Barnes, it severed its link with the West End and David was never really part of the Mayfair art world. He did not pander to fashionable taste and, like many of his artists, he followed his own instincts for better or for worse. He disliked many aspects of the London art world and the sharp practices that he saw around him amongst both dealers and auctioneers, always maintaining that he was not a dealer – he promoted and supported artists but never speculated in their work. In his own words, he continued 'to paddle his canoe' for forty years, selecting his own artists and making his own judgements.

David never had any illusions about the difficulties and frustrations of running a gallery. He realised that there were many easier and more effective ways of making money. Had he stayed with Shell or within the PR business in general, he would probably have enjoyed more money, longer holidays and a well-paid retirement. In fact he took only short holidays, constantly telephoning the gallery to see how an exhibition was progressing, and he never retired. His last one-man exhibition was that of Tom Coates in late 2001; it was followed by the most successful Christmas show ever with eighty-five pictures sold. David worked right up to the last moment, meeting clients, selling pictures, arranging the gallery programme for the forthcoming years and achieving his own ambition – 'never to retire'.

For David, the New Grafton Gallery was a passion and a way of life rather than a business. He only showed work that he liked and respected, and never took on an artist because he thought the work would sell. He realised that it takes time to promote an artist and was always prepared to subsidise exhibitions in the knowledge that one day his faith in a painter would be justified and rewarded. This approach inspired loyalty in both artist and collector, a loyalty which David expected, and from artists, even demanded. When an artist left the gallery to join another, David would feel personally upset, and it was probably this close personal relationship with the artists that lies at the heart of his success. Equally he liked to establish close rapport with his clients, many of whom became personal friends. He always believed that he was dealing with people rather than with art.

There are many who, like David Wolfers, believe that British figurative painting since the Second World War is amongst the best in Western art. It has variety, sincerity, technique and is not constantly looking over its shoulder towards fashion; nor is it dominated, or indeed intimidated, by past artistic greatness and reputation. David Wolfers and his gallery played an important part in establishing, nurturing and promoting the artists of this creative period in Britain. David Wolfers was to his period what Ambroise Vollard was to Impressionism.

List of exhibitions 1968–2002

Grafton Street, London W1

1968
Artists of Today and Tomorrow
Vile Bodies
Presents

1969
The Nude
Mary Kessell
Olwyn Bowey and Ben Levene
Horace Mann Livens
Fire and Water
Eighteenth and Nineteenth-Century
  English Watercolours, Paintings
  and Drawings
Alan Dodd
When the Going Was Good
Vincent Butler
Christmas Show

1970
New Year Exhibition
Dick Lee
John O'Connor
Josef Herman
Fred Uhlman
English Painting 1914–1945
Hermione Hammond
Charles Duranty and Artists of
  Today and Tomorrow Part 1
Harold Cheeseman and Artists of
  Today and Tomorrow Part 2
Three Decades
Alan Dodd, Jean Boswell and
  Smaller Paintings for Christmas

1971
David Boyd
Clothilde Peploe
Ken Howard
Olwyn Bowey and Jean Cooke
Florence Martin and Gallery Selection
Edmund Fairfax-Lucy and Artists of
  Today and Tomorrow Part 1
Michael D'Aguilar and Artists of
  Today and Tomorrow Part 2
30 Years 1909–1939
Martinez Novillo
The City of London

1972
Dick Lee
John O'Connor
Peter Greenham
Reynolds Stone
Margaret Green
Chaim Stephenson and Artists of
  Today and Tomorrow
Eileen Hogan
Alan Dodd
English Painting 1900–1940
Vanishing London

1973
English Drawing 1900–1940
Anthony Eyton
David Boyd
Penelope Makins
David Remfry
Fifth Anniversary Mixed Show
Lloyd Rees
English Painting 1900–1940
Clothilde Peploe

1974
English Drawing 1900–1940
Ken Howard
Carel Weight
Christopher Hall
Fred Dubery
Jane Dowling
Carolyn Trant
Artists of Today and Tomorrow
John O'Connor
English Painting 1900–1940
Dick Lee

1975
English Drawing 1900–1940
Reynolds Stone
Edward Ardizzone
Peter Greenham
Oliver Campion
Cedric Morris
Artists of Today and Tomorrow
Mary Fedden
English Painting 1900–1940
Anonymous

1976
Bernard Dunstan
Catherine Alexander, Kathleen Hale
  and Siddig El Nigoumi
John Verney

Bond Street, London W1

Ken Howard
Christopher Hall
Artists of Today and Tomorrow
Edmund Fairfax-Lucy, Maurice Sheppard
  and Colin Hayes
English Painting 1900–1940
Carel Weight

1977
New Year Bargains
John O'Connor
Jeremy Holt
Julian Trevelyan
Intimate Impressions
Artists of Today and Tomorrow
Orovida Pissarro and Her Ancestors
English Painting and Drawing 1900–1940
Mary Fedden

1978
New Year Bargains
Zdzislaw Ruszkowski
Reynolds Stone
Clotilde Peploe
John Nash
Jane Dowling and Artists of
  Today and Tomorrow
Patricio Goycolea
Christopher Hall
Ken Howard
Dick Lee

1979
English Painting and Drawing 1900–1940
James Bolivar Manson –
  Centenary Exhibition
Peter Greenham
Elizabeth Sorrell
Helen Binyon and Artists of
  Today and Tomorrow
Ken Howard

Moy Keightley and Maurice Sheppard
Edna Clarke-Hall and English Painting
Sheila Fell

1980
Morwenna Thistlewaite
Bernard Myers
Mary Fedden
John Nash
John O'Connor
John Aldridge
Artists of Today and Tomorrow
Carel Weight
English Painting and Drawing 1900–1940
Mary Mabbutt

1981
John Hastings
Edward Ardizzone
John Nash
Christopher Hall
Cherryl Fountain and Margaret Neve
Artists of Today and Tomorrow
Ann Arnold
Oliver Campion
Ken Howard
Henry Lamb
At the Bath Festival with Nash, Howard,
 Fedden, Hall, Sergeant, Arnold

1982
Hugh MacKinnon
Lady Edna Clarke Hall (1879–1979)
Clothilde Peploe
Mary Fedden
Artists of Today and Tomorrow
English Drawing and Painting
Jane Dowling

49 Church Road, Barnes SW13

Opening Exhibition
Dick Lee
Joanna Carrington
Smaller Paintings for Christmas
 and the New Year

1983
Moy Keightley
Lamb, Spencer, Nash and
 Edna Clarke Hall

Julian Trevelyan
Peter Greenham
Christopher Hall
Fred Cuming
Jacqueline Rizvi
Artists of Today and Tomorrow
Gwyneth Johnstone
John Nash Woodcuts and
 Crayon Drawings, Maurice Percival
Paul Newland
Smaller Paintings

1984
Alex Lumley and Anthea Craigmyle
John Piper 80th Birthday – Watercolours
 and lithographs
John Armstrong (1893–1973)
Ken Howard
Mary Fedden
Josephine Trotter
Artists of Today and Tomorrow
Christa Gaa and Peter Kuhfeld
Marie Hugo
André Bicat
Henry Lamb and Some Contemporaries
Smaller Paintings

1985
Cartoons and Watercolours
 by Barry Fantoni
Anne Graham
Julian Trevelyan
Dick Lee
Fred Cuming
Teachers at the Royal Academy Schools
 from Rushbury to Greenham
Artists of Today and Tomorrow
Duncan Oppenheim
Keith Vaughan
Ann Arnold
Smaller Paintings

1986
Reg Gammon
Hitchens and Heron
Mary Fedden
Ken Howard
Festival of Britain Painters
 Thirty Years On
Artists of Today and Tomorrow
Cherryl Fountain and Haidee Becker
Peter Kuhfeld

Alex Lumley
Peter Greenham and Jane Dowling
Smaller Paintings

1987
David Imms
Oliver Campion
Fred Cuming
Keith Vaughan
Josephine Trotter
John Nash
Dick Lee
Summer Show
Julian Trevelyan
Elinor Bellingham-Smith,
 Graham Hurdwood, Paul Newland,
 Martin Yeoman
John Aldridge
Christmas Show

1988
Anthea Craigmyle and Irene Wise
Bernard Myers and Alex Lumley
Ken Howard
Tom Coates
Duncan Oppenheim
Fred Cuming
Artists of Today and Tomorrow
Reg Gammon
Mary Fedden
Oliver Campion
Christmas Show

1989
John O'Connor
David Imms
Jacqueline Williams
John Nash and Henry Lamb
Elinor Bellingham-Smith
Jane Dowling
Tom Coates
Summer Show
Fred Dubery
Elisabeth Frink
Peter Greenham
Fred Cuming and Christmas Show

1990
Kristin Charlesworth
Paul Riley, Neale Worley,
 Michael Corkrey
Fred Cuming

Ken Howard
Christa Gaa
Carel Weight, Colin Hayes,
 Olwyn Bowey, Mick Rooney
Martin Yeoman
Moy Keightley and Artists of
 Today and Tomorrow
Jacqueline Williams
Richard Pikesley
Oliver Campion
Smaller Paintings for Christmas

1991
Reg Gammon
Joanna Carrington and
 Christopher Mason
Tom Coates
Julian Bailey
Lucy Dynevor
Josephine Trotter
Jane Dowling and Peter Greenham
Artists of Today and Tomorrow
Jason Bowyer
Paul Riley
Bernard Myers
Fred Cuming
Smaller Paintings for Christmas

1992
David Imms and Anthea Craigmyle
Gill Watkiss
Sir Duncan Oppenheim and
 Sarah Chalmers
John Nash CBE RA (1893–1977) and
 Sarah Spencer
Christa Gaa
Martin Yeoman and Summer Show
Fred Dubery
Oliver Campion
Jacqueline Williams
Ann Arnold
Watercolours of Venice by Ken Howard
 and Smaller Paintings

1993
Reg Gammon
Tom Coates
Dick Lee
Ken Howard
25th Anniversary Show
Gus Cummins and Alex Lumley
Carel Weight, Mick Rooney,

Helen Roeder and Cyril Reason
Peter Greenham CBE RA (1909–1992)
 Memorial Exhibition
Fred Cuming
Smaller Paintings for Christmas

1994
Christa Gaa (1937–1992)
Julian Bailey
Pip Todd Warmoth
Josephine Trotter
20th Century British Painting and
 Drawing and Woodcuts by John Nash
Reg Gammon Centenary Exhibition
Artists of Today and Tomorrow
Jacqueline Williams
Sarah Spencer and Sarah Chalmers
Paul Riley
Richard Pikesley
Smaller Paintings for Christmas

1995
Clive McCartney
Jason Bowyer
Tom Coates
Ken Howard
Henrietta Young and Laura Matthews
Artists of Today and Tomorrow
Michael Smee
Oliver Campion
Fred Cuming RA
Smaller Paintings for Christmas

1996
Christa Gaa (1937–1992)
Julian Bailey and Susan-Jayne Hocking
Jane Dowling
Pip Todd Warmoth
Carel Weight, Mick Rooney,
 Gus Cummins and Helen Roeder
John Piper CH (1903–1992)
Artists of Today and Tomorrow
Ruth Stage and Jacqueline Williams
Josef Herman OBE RA
Colin Hayes RA PRBA A Retrospective
Smaller Paintings for Christmas

1997
John Nash
Jason Bowyer
Tom Coates
Susan Wilson and James Fotheringhame

Fred Cuming RA
Richard Pikesley and Mary Jackson
Christopher Hall and Alex Lumley
Summer Show
20th Century Paintings and Drawings
Mark Adlington and Alasdair Rennie
Sue Campion
Ruth Stage
Ken Howard
Christmas Show

1998
Lliam Spencer
Jane Dowling and John O'Connor
Susan Jayne Hocking
Josef Herman
Pip Todd Warmoth
Colin Hayes
Tom Coates
Artists of Today and Tomorrow
Gus Cummins, Edmund Fairfax-Lucy and
 Mary Mabbutt
Oliver Campion
Fred Dubery
Fred Cuming RA
Smaller Paintings for Christmas

1999
Reg Gammon (1894–1997)
 Memorial Exhibition
Jason Bowyer and Laura Matthews
Mark Adlington and Sarah Chalmers
Sue Campion
Alison Sloga
Ruth Stage
Artists of Today and Tomorrow
Richard Pikesley
Peter Brook
John Nash
Smaller Paintings for Christmas

2000
The Box Show:
 Young Contemporary Artists
Susan-Jayne Hocking
Julian Bailey, Jenny Grevatte, Jax Martin-
 Betts, Laura Matthews, Sarah Spencer
 and Ruth Stage
Pip Todd Warmoth
Tom Coates
Artists of Today and Tomorrow
Alex Lumley and Jacqueline Williams

Anthea Craigmyle
Fred Cuming RA
Ken Howard
Smaller Paintings for Christmas

2001
Alison Sloga
Jason Bowyer and Mary Mabbutt
Ruth Stage
Richard Pikesley
Mark Adlington and Fred Dubery
Sue Campion
Josef Herman OBE RA (1911–2000)
  Memorial Show
Artists of Today and Tomorrow
The Egg Tempera Society
Peter Brook
Oliver Campion (1928–2000)
  Memorial Show
Tom Coates
Smaller Paintings for Christmas

2002
John Nash and Sarah Spencer
Susan-Jayne Hocking
Julian Bailey and Ann Shrager
Ann Arnold, Alex Lumley and
  Alasdair Rennie
Pip Todd Warmoth
Artists of Today and Tomorrow
Richard Pikesley
Anthea Craigmyle
Fred Cuming RA
Smaller Paintings for Christmas

Artists of the Portrait Centre 1968–2002

Painters
Jean Boswell
Olwyn Bowey RA
William Bowyer RA
Robert Buhler RA
Oliver Campion
Mary Carter
Tom Coates
Jeffrey Courtney
Annabel Cullen
Deidre Daines
Jane Dowling
Helen Elwes
Tom Epsley
Margaret Foreman
Bridget Garrett
Patrick George
Peter Greenham CBE RA
Roger de Grey PRA
Colin Hayes
Peter Kuhfeld
Ishbel McWhirter
Laura Matthews
Sarah Niccolini
Michael Noakes
David Remfry
Alasdair Rennie
Hans Schwarz
Rupert Shephard
Ruskin Spear CBE RA
Lincoln Taber
Daphne Todd
Carel Weight CH RA
John Whittall
Tom Wise
Walter Woodington
Juliet Wood
Martin Yeoman
Henrietta Young

Sculptors
Angela Connor
Karin Jonzen
Patricia Rae
Ivor Roberts-Jones CBE RA
Jill Tweed

Index